Chyka
HOME

To my Darling Bruce, Chessie and BJ.

Thank you for always being there for me and supporting everything I do. You are my world, and without you, I wouldn't be the woman I am today.

Chyka HOME

Chyka Keebaugh

hardie grant books

INTRODUCTION

" As a child, I loved having stories read to me and truly embraced the world of make-believe. I spent endless hours in my grandparents' beautiful garden making my own magic potions and perfumes using crushed up flower petals and soap. All I ever wanted was my own secret garden and a table to set up afternoon tea for my dolls and friends.

As I got older, my grandmothers taught me so much about house-keeping, cooking and flower arrangements. From them, I inherited the knowledge of how to create a beautiful and happy home. I know they are both smiling down at me now, thinking, 'She did listen!'

For many years, I have worked to create and realise other people's dreams. Now, my own dream has come to fruition: my whole life, I have been drawn to books, so writing and creating a book has always been on my bucket list. To have completed my first book on home styling and entertaining in sync with the seasons is a dream come true.

I am incredibly excited to share my tips and tricks on styling and organising your home, along with indoor and outdoor DIY projects, suggestions for entertaining friends (complete with delicious, simple recipes) and inspiration for thoughtful little gifts.

I love changing my house throughout the year, embracing the colours and produce that nature has on offer. My home is my favourite place in the world. Making it inviting and comfortable year-round is my idea of bliss, whether it is by filling it with the colours and scents of blossoms in spring, letting in the warm breeze on a long summer's night, styling with autumnal shades as the days get shorter again, or adding extra blankets, throws and flickering candles for warmth in winter.

The possibilities when styling are endless, from colour-blocking books to displaying candles, knick-knacks and jewellery – find your personal style using items around the house.

Nowadays, we are all seriously busy juggling a million and one things, and it is easy to forget about the little things that matter in life and that make us happy. Spending time with family and friends is the greatest luxury, and entertaining is the perfect way to get everyone together for that long overdue catch up.

Having friends over for dinner should be fun, and with a little organising, it doesn't have to become a major production. We all become stuck in a rut sometimes – I hope that this book helps you to see and do things differently.

Chyka Home is a book full of practical tips, but also a book to inspire you, to make you think outside the box. My dream is for you to look through your cupboards and find those old teacups or pots that haven't been used forever and give them a new lease on life – relive old memories and cherish what you have in the moment.

With love,

Chyka

SPRING

14 Introduction

17 Bulbs & Blooms
18 My love of bulbs
20 Spring blossom table
25 Passionfruit Mojito
26 The perfect spring posy
29 Make your own flower preserve

31 Lemons
32 Lemon table
34 Lemon butter
37 Homemade lemonade
37 Preserved lemons
38 Cleaning with lemons

41 Feathers & Eggs
42 Feather your nest
44 The perfect roast chicken
46 Build a nest egg

49 Spring Clean
50 Nature's way
53 Simple stain removers
54 Freshen up your bedroom
56 The guest room
58 How to fold a fitted sheet
59 Homemade linen water

SUMMER

64 Introduction

67 Roses
68 A summer romance
72 The semi-naked cake
77 Rose cocktail
77 Rose tea
78 How to dry roses
81 How to press flowers

83 Tomatoes
84 A green thumb's birthday
88 Terrific tomatoes
90 Bloody Mary
93 Tomato and ricotta tarts
93 Homemade tomato sauce

95 Peruvian Barbecue
96 Welcome to Peru
99 Pisco Sour
100 Peruvian feast
102 Avocado, tomato and cheese salad
103 Quinoa, avocado and sweet corn salad
104 Pollo a la brasa (grilled chicken)
104 Thyme and crispy shallot potatoes
106 Grilled lamb chops with herbs and spices
107 Peruvian green sauce

109 Outdoors
110 Summer sunshine
114 Get cleaning while the sun shines

CONTE

AUTUMN

120 Introduction

123 Darling Dahlias
124 Tea among the dahlias
126 How to make a dahlia block
128 Decorating with dahlias

131 Vegetables
133 Pumpkin table
134 The perfect roast vegetables
135 Roasted root vegetable salad
137 Kale Caesar salad
137 Autumn artichoke dip

139 Leaves
140 Autumnal crunch
142 Greek dolmades
144 The gift of autumn

147 Around The House
148 The kitchen
150 Display your collections in clusters
152 The pantry
154 The laundry
156 Washing your woollies
158 Dressing room

WINTER

166 Introduction

169 Orchids
170 Orchids on the table
172 Winter wonders
175 Whiskey bar
176 Espresso Old Fashioned

179 Olives
180 A picnic in the olive grove
183 Olive tapenade
184 Lemon and rosemary olive oil cake
186 Infused olive oil

189 Mushrooms
190 A whimsical mushroom table setting
192 Common mushroom types
194 Pickled mushrooms
196 Mushroom pizza
198 Garlic confit
201 Mushroom pancetta spaghetti
201 Mushroom feta tart
202 Meringue mushrooms

205 Books & Fireplaces
206 Styling your home with books
208 Create a masculine office space
210 Save me a spot by the fire
212 Firewood
214 Candles

218 Index
223 About Chyka
223 Thank You

NTS

SPR

ING

SPRING IS THE TIME OF BLOSSOMS GALORE

" Spring is my favourite season, without a doubt. Seeing winter's bare branches burst with new leaves and buds, and watching daffodils, jonquils, hyacinths and tulips come out in all their glory always puts a little spring in my step. There's no excuse not to have a beautiful bunch of flowers in your house at this time of year.

It's time to pack the winter woollies away, spring clean and brighten up your living spaces with everything the season has to offer. Leave those doors wide open and feel the fresh breeze drift through your home.

BULBS & BLOOMS

" The thing I love the most about spring is flowering bulbs. It seems magical to me that these little babies are hiding under the cold, wet soil and then, suddenly, POP! With a little help from the sun, out of the ground they come with all that colour and the most heavenly smell. If you have ever travelled through Europe in spring, you would have seen masses of colour, from the smallest planter box filled to the brim with flowering bulbs, to endless fields full of blooms.

MY LOVE
OF BULBS

Buying flowering bulbs at the nursery and transplanting them from pot to vase (soil and all) is a gorgeous way to show these blooms off, while a bunch of jonquils and fresh herbs tied together with a simple ribbon is a pretty way to make a spring bouquet. If you are looking for a dramatic idea for giving a bunch of flowers to a friend, wash the soil off some bulbs and present the flowers with the bulbs still attached.

" Bulbs are attractive, long-lasting plants to have in the house and can be displayed in a variety of ways.

HOW TO GROW BULBS AT HOME

◈ Choose a pot with good drainage and place some pebbles in the bottom. Fill the pot with potting mix (a specialist bulb mix if possible) and plant the bulb with its root facing down.

◈ Put the pot in a cool, dark place and keep the soil moist to encourage root growth.

◈ When bulbs begin to bloom, keep them near a window, but not in direct sunlight – the sun can burn them and make the foliage fade.

◈ Check your soil once or twice a week, watering only when it feels dry. Don't let your pot sit in a wet tray, as the soil will absorb too much liquid.

◈ After your bulb has flowered, remove the flower head by snipping it off at the base, leaving the stem.

◈ Once your bulb's foliage and flowers have faded, you can either move your pot outdoors or transplant the bulb to a well-drained garden. Bulbs will remain dormant through summer, autumn and winter but will bloom again the following spring.

SPRING BLOSSOM TABLE

Celebrating spring is something I love, but celebrating spring at my favourite florist is even better!

Flowers Vasette in Melbourne has been my go-to florist for decades and is one of my absolute favourite places to visit. If being among an abundance of colourful spring flowers is your idea of heaven, this is the perfect store for you. The smell, colour and sheer volume of blooms is the most incredible assault on the senses and goes hand in hand with my favourite little saying: 'more is more is more'. Because, when it comes to flowers, you can never have too many.

I used every type of flower I could get my hands on for this opulent setting, making sure I kept each variety together and displayed them at different heights to create a sea of blooms.

I knew the flowers were going to have serious wow factor, but I also loved the idea of emphasising the green. I found some wide, green-and-white striped fabric and had it made into a tablecloth. I set the table with layered large white plates and green patterned napkins to make it look even happier. To me, spring is all about new growth, and while there are flowers and colours galore here, the green centres the table and brings everything together.

> **"** There is so much to choose from when it comes to cutlery. For this setting, I found some old cutlery at the market and dipped the handles into white paint.

Painting cutlery is a fun project – you can choose any colour that works with your table setting. It won't last forever, but it certainly looks fantastic. I really wanted to highlight the white on the table so I also used white water glasses. Continuing my market theme, I used a collection of cut-glass vases to create an eclectic look and kept all my colours and flowers separate, which gives the setting a much stronger look.

Place cards are a great way to show that a little bit of extra time and thought has gone into the table. For this setting, I reversed the usual white card with green writing, to a green card with white writing, which I think looks bolder and more creative. Best of all, once the meal is over you can tie each guest's place card to a lovely spring posy so they can take a little piece of spring home with them.

PASSIONFRUIT MOJITO

This is the perfect refreshing cocktail to serve to your guests on arrival.

crushed ice

juice of 1 lime

1½ teaspoons unrefined cane sugar

8–10 fresh mint leaves (torn),
plus an extra sprig to garnish

1 large, ripe passionfruit, pulped
(or 1 tablespoon passionfruit purée)

60 ml (2 fl oz/¼ cup) white rum

30–60 ml (1–2 fl oz) chilled soda water
(club soda)

½ passionfruit, to garnish (optional)

–

SERVES 1

Fill a tall glass three-quarters of the way with crushed ice.

Combine the lime juice, sugar, mint, passionfruit and rum in a cocktail shaker and shake for 30 seconds, until the passionfruit seeds separate.

Pour into the prepared glass and stir, then top with soda water and more ice if needed.

Garnish with a sprig of mint and the passionfruit half, if desired, and serve.

THE PERFECT SPRING POSY

 Spring is the ideal time to go to the market and find buckets of beautiful coloured flowers to make into a posy. I don't usually like to mix blooms, but who can resist at this time of year? Whether you're making a bouquet to sit on your kitchen bench, or to give to a friend, have fun putting it all together. Go all out with the colours, or stick to one palette. You can't go wrong either way.

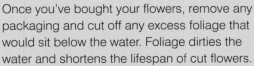

Once you've bought your flowers, remove any packaging and cut off any excess foliage that would sit below the water. Foliage dirties the water and shortens the lifespan of cut flowers.

Before I get started, I like to keep all my flowers in separate piles, cut to the same length. Start with larger flowers, like kale, and constantly turn the arrangement so no one area gets more attention than another, then slowly layer up with more delicate flowers (such as tulips) to create a whimsical feel. Smaller flowers, like hyacinths and hellebores, are perfect for filling in gaps. Finally, bring it all together with a beautiful ribbon.

SIMPLE TIPS FOR FLOWER ARRANGEMENTS

❖ Don't cram too many flowers into your vase. They need room to breathe air and drink water.

❖ Replace the water every 2–3 days to ensure healthy blooms.

❖ Drooping flowers should be recut and put into fresh water.

❖ If a flower is wilting, toss it! Don't let one bloom ruin the lot.

❖ Your flowers should live in a happy place away from draughts and heat.

BULK OUT YOUR SPRING POSY WITH HERBS

❖ A large bunch of mint looks great with blooms that have soft petals, such as hellebores and lilacs.

❖ A structured herb like rosemary goes well with tall-stemmed flowers like daffodils or irises.

❖ A small, mixed-bloom posy looks fabulous with some thyme added in.

How to prepare flowers

Kale: Remove any foliage that would sit below the water and cut the stems at a 45-degree angle to allow more water to be absorbed. Kale dirties water quickly, so the water will need to be changed daily or it will get smelly.

Tulips: Remove excess foliage and cut the stems on a 45-degree angle. Tulips continue to grow in water so trim the stems 2–5 cm (¾–2 in) every couple of days. If the flower starts to droop, prick the stem directly under the head of the bulb with a pin to remove any air bubbles, which cause tulips to droop. If your florist provided a sachet of flower food, mix it in with your vase water. Alternatively, you can add a teaspoon of sugar or a dash of lemonade.

Hellebores: Cut the stems on a 45-degree angle and strip away any leaves that would sit below the water. Hellebores need to be seared as soon as possible by lowering the stem ends (about 2 cm/¾ in) into boiling water for 30 seconds. You can then arrange the flowers in any pattern you like.

DID YOU KNOW?

Fruit and flowers are not friends. Don't keep your flowers near a fruit bowl or they may not open. Fruit omits a gas that flowers don't like, so, in revolt, they don't bloom as brightly and will die faster.

Preparing flower stems

There are generally five types of flower stems, each with different needs. Understanding what type of stem your flower has and how it should be treated will help you prepare your cut flowers properly and ensure their longevity.

Hearty (marigolds): Flowers with hearty stems need to be cut on the diagonal to absorb maximum water. Leave them in lukewarm water for about an hour before arranging them in a bouquet.

Hollow (hollyhocks, dahlias, delphiniums, lupins): Flowers with a hollow stem need to be filled with water. To do this, turn each flower upside down and pour water into the open cavity of the stalk, then put them straight into a vase of water. The trapped water will keep the stem strong and straight.

Soft (freesias, hellebores, anemones, poppies): Bulb flowers have delicate stems. Cut them just above the white bulb, then place them into a vase of cold water.

Woody (snowballs, dogwood, lilac, eucalyptus): Flowers with woody stems need to be split by cutting an X into the base of the stem with secateurs or a sharp knife. This creates more surface area to absorb water.

Milky (kale, euphorbia, ficus): Stems that ooze sap into the water can clog the stem and stop water from being absorbed. You have two choices: either dip the cut end of the flower into boiling water for 30 seconds or apply a flame from a match or candle to the cut stem for about 30 seconds to seal the base. Each time you trim the flowers, they will need to be seared again.

MAKE YOUR OWN FLOWER PRESERVE

This simple mixture will help keep your flowers looking fresh.

1 teaspoon sugar

1 teaspoon household bleach

2 teaspoons lemon or lime juice

1 litre (34 fl oz/4 cups) lukewarm water

–

MAKES ABOUT 1 LITRE (34 FL OZ/4 CUPS)

Combine all the ingredients in a jug and stir until the sugar has dissolved.

Stir the preserve into the vase water at a ratio of 1 part preserve to 4 parts water.

Leftover preserve can be stored in an airtight container for up to 3 months.

LEMONS

"I love lemon trees in spring, when their branches are abundant with bright yellow fruit. If you're lucky enough to have a tree of your own, it will provide you with armloads of lemons that can be used for cooking, cleaning, drinking, preserving and, of course, decorating.

LEMON TABLE

This lemon-themed table centrepiece was inspired by a collection of beautiful plates I bought while on holiday in Capri. These handmade beauties are the real heroes of the table setting, so I needed the table centrepiece to be simple. And simple it is.

To recreate it, all you need to do is gather a collection of lemons still attached to their branches. Don't fuss too much over their shape, just go for branches with lush, green leaves. Layer the branches down the centre of the table and fill the gaps with extra lemons. You can cut some in half for extra effect and aroma. Tie a place card to a lemon and place it on each guest's plate. How beautiful, simple and effective is that?

LEMON BUTTER

There is nothing better than homemade lemon butter; its flavour is the perfect balance of sweet and tart. This recipe is super simple and you can use it in so many ways – piped into mini tartlets or spread on cakes or hot crumpets, to name just a few.

125 g (4½ oz) unsalted butter, chopped

230 g (8 oz/1 cup) caster (superfine) sugar

4 eggs, lightly beaten

finely grated zest and juice of 2 lemons

—

MAKES 500 G (1 LB 2 OZ)

Combine the butter and sugar in a microwave-safe bowl and microwave on high for 2 minutes. Stir well.

In a separate bowl, whisk the eggs with the lemon zest and juice until combined.

Quickly whisk the egg mixture into the hot butter and sugar until combined.

Microwave on high for 4 minutes until thick, whisking well every 1 minute.

Cool, then pour into a sterilised glass jar (see page 37 on how to sterilise jars) or an airtight container and refrigerate for up to 2 weeks.

"Lemon Butter"

Makes 500 grams.

Ingredients

25 grams unsalted butter, chopped
1 cup caster sugar
4 eggs lightly beaten
Finely grated rind & juice of
2 lemons

Method
(1) Combine butter & sugar in a
microwave - safe bowl. Microwave
on high for two minutes & stir well.
(2) Whisk eggs, lemon juice & rind
in a separate bowl until
combined.
(3) Quickly whisk egg mixture
into the hot butter to combine.
(4) Microwave on high for four
minutes until thick, whisking
in well at 1 minute intervals.
(5) Cool refridgerate up to 2 weeks.

HOMEMADE LEMONADE

My kids loved having a lemonade stand outside our house when they were young. The joy they had making and selling the sweet syrup was too cute for words and it was such a treat to see cars stop to buy their homemade lemonade and biscuits. This simple lemonade recipe is easy to make and great on its own with plenty of ice. For the adults, add some gin for that perfect summer cocktail.

230 g (8 oz/1 cup) caster (superfine) sugar

250 ml (8½ fl oz/1 cup) water

250 ml (8½ fl oz/1 cup) freshly squeezed lemon juice

750 ml (25½ fl oz/3 cups) soda water (club soda)

ice

–

MAKES 500 ML (17 FL OZ/2 CUPS) OF SYRUP

Place the sugar and water in a saucepan and stir over a low heat until the sugar has dissolved.

Allow to cool, then stir in the lemon juice.

To serve, pour the syrup into a tall glass and top with chilled soda water and ice. Adjust the syrup–soda ratio to your taste.

PRESERVED LEMONS

Gift-giving is such a special thing to do, so why not make up a batch of preserved lemons to give away? They taste amazing with chicken or in a salad.

5 unwaxed lemons

80 g (2¾ oz/¼ cup) coarse salt, plus more if desired

3 whole cloves

6 whole coriander seeds

4 whole black peppercorns

1 cinnamon stick

1 bay leaf

–

MAKES 200 G (7 OZ)

Cut each lemon into quarters, leaving the segments connected at the bottom. Generously sprinkle salt on the exposed flesh, then push each lemon back together.

Boil a medium mason jar in water for 10 minutes to sterilise it and let it air-dry on a clean tea (dish) towel. Once dry, put a tablespoon of salt in the bottom of the jar and pack the lemons in, one by one, adding the cloves, coriander seeds, peppercorns and a bit more salt, between each lemon. As you add each lemon, press it down to release its juice and make room for more fruit.

Add the cinnamon stick and bay leaf last. Ensure the lemons are covered by juice (add extra freshly squeezed lemon juice if required), but leave a 1 cm (½ in) gap to the top. Seal the jar.

Store in a warm place and gently shake the jar each day to distribute the salt and juice. The lemons will be ready to eat after 30 days, and can be stored for up to 1 year.

CLEANING WITH LEMONS

I love the versatility of lemons – did you know they are amazing for cleaning? Their acidity breaks through grease and oil, and there is no cleaner or fresher smell than a freshly picked lemon that's just been cut in half.

How to clean with lemon

Ants: Ants hate lemon, so rubbing a lemon half along the areas they trail along will keep them away. Scatter a few rinds where they are entering to detract them, too.

Butcher's block: Butcher's block stained? Sprinkle some coarse salt on the stain and rub some lemon juice in. Let it sit overnight, then wipe away. This is perfect for small, light stains.

Fridge: Cut a lemon in half and wipe your fridge with the cut half to help eliminate odours. You can also leave a cloth soaked in fresh lemon juice, or a small container full of it, in the fridge for 1–3 days to help remove odours.

Garbage disposal: Throw a few rinds down your garbage disposal for a quick freshen up.

Microwave: Cut a lemon in half and squeeze the juice into a microwave-safe bowl. Add 125 ml (4 fl oz/½ cup) of water and the squeezed lemon half. Microwave for 3–5 minutes, then remove the bowl. Wait for 5 minutes then wipe it out.

Plastic: For stubborn stains in plastic containers, rub the insides with a lemon half before rinsing with warm water. This will help reduce the stain and smell.

Wooden chopping board: Cut a lemon in half and dip the cut half into coarse salt. Wet the board with warm water and scrub away. Once it's looking clean and fresh again, put it out in the sun to dry.

USING LEMONS IN FOOD PREPARATION

❖ Squeeze some lemon juice on the cut side of an avocado and it will stay green for longer.

❖ When boiling vegetables like potato and cauliflower, which tend to brown, add a squeeze of lemon to the water to keep them white.

❖ When cooking rice, add a spoonful of lemon juice to the water to stop the rice becoming gluggy. Fluff with a fork before serving.

FEATHERS & EGGS

" Spring, to me, says new life and growth: little chicks are hatching and the air is filled with birdsong. I love to capture this beautiful awakening of nature in my styling and entertaining – and how better to celebrate spring than by referencing where it all begins?

FEATHER YOUR NEST

 What I love about this outdoor table setting is that you can avoid using a tablecloth. Simply go to your nursery and buy a couple of bags of moss to create a lush, green covering. I also added potted pansies and birds' nests filled with quail eggs that I picked up at my local market, to create an earthy, fresh-growth look.

I included some dark, modern plates in this setting to contrast with the softness of the green moss. Teaming them with scrunched, unironed linen napkins and black cutlery balances the colour of the quail eggs and creates a really clean look. I love the idea of this being an outdoor table, but it could work on any table in your home.

The grey, green and neutral colours of the eggs are a stunning feature and, for an extra touch, I've added some little clip-on birds. These double as something you can give to your guests as they leave and ties in perfectly with our feather-and-egg theme.

Naturally, a roast chicken is the perfect dish to serve in this setting. All you have to do is stuff it, cook it and serve it.

THE PERFECT ROAST CHICKEN

1 × 1.6 kg (3½ lb) whole chicken

sea salt

freshly ground black pepper

butter (optional)

3 lemons, halved

small sprig of thyme

sage, rosemary and thyme, to garnish

—

SERVES 4

Preheat the oven to 230°C (450°F). For a more succulent roast, remove the chicken from the refrigerator and bring to room temperature before cooking.

Season the chicken inside and out with salt and pepper. Smear the skin with butter if you are feeling a little decadent.

Squeeze 1 lemon over the chicken and stuff the remaining lemon halves into the cavity, along with the sprig of thyme.

Place the chicken, breast-side up, in a deep roasting tin.

Roast the chicken for approximately 50 minutes, or until the skin is golden brown and the juices run clear when a skewer is inserted into the thickest part of the meat. Baste the chicken with the pan juices halfway through to keep the meat juicy.

BUILD A
NEST EGG

> This DIY bird's nest is a great spring project that's perfect as a gift, or for decorating your home. I love giving these out as housewarming presents – everybody knows that moving into a new space is all about feathering your nest.

What you'll need

dodo vine

florist wire

fresh moss

baby-sized feathers

–

Buy your dodo vine, fresh moss and florist wire from your local florist. Baby feathers can be found at your local craft store.

Take a bunch of dodo vine and fashion it into a bird's nest by twisting and pulling the vines until you're happy with the shape. Dodo vine is sturdy, easy to manipulate and holds its shape well.

Weave florist wire around the nest to help it hold its shape. Use as much or as little as you need, and keep your nest rustic and natural.

Once you are happy with your nest, place some moss inside the nest and decorate it with feathers.

Display your nest on a bookshelf or under a glass dome.

SPRING CLEAN

❝ I know I'm ready to embrace spring when the sun starts to come out and we can leave the back door open for a little warmth. This is the perfect time to let in the spring breeze and freshen up the house with a spring clean – remove that winter dust, and get ready to enjoy the new season!

NATURE'S WAY

I am obsessed with cleaning, and spring is when it all happens in our house. As important as it is to make your house feel fresh and germ-free, it's also important to not use too many chemicals. Our grandmothers had the right idea using natural products for cleaning. Apart from smelling great, they are better for the environment, too.

Cleaning the natural way

Vinegar: To remove watermarks from windows and mirrors, mix one part vinegar and two parts water.

To remove dirt from glass, add 1 tablespoon of dishwashing detergent, then wash your windows and buff with a dry cloth.

For a natural fabric softener, mix one part white vinegar and two parts water, then add to the final rinse cycle.

Lemons: Cut a lemon in half and rub it directly onto brass, copper or chrome to make it shine.

To clean tile grout, squeeze some lemon juice onto an old toothbrush and scrub away. You can also rub a cut lemon on shower glass to remove hard-water stains.

Got an oil-stained shirt? Rub half a lemon onto the stain and watch the oil break down.

Bicarbonate of soda (baking soda): Don't be put off by tarnished silver, there are a few natural ways to get that shine back.

Line a bowl with aluminium foil and fill it with 1 litre (34 fl oz/4 cups) of water and 1 tablespoon of baking soda. Drop your silverware in for ten seconds then remove with tongs and buff; simple. Leaving a few sticks of chalk in your silver drawer will absorb moisture and prevent tarnishing.

HOW TO CLEAN CRYSTAL

1. Before you start, line your sink with a tea towel and fill it with hot soapy water. Move your tap head out of the way so you don't accidentally break any crystal on it.

2. Clean your crystal with a long-handled, soft-bristled scrubbing brush. Make sure you get into all the grooves and crevices.

3. Rinse with hot water and leave to dry.

4. Store your glasses upside down. Never stack them on top of each other.

QUICK CLEANING HACKS

Get your cleaning jobs done quickly with these time-saving tricks.

- **Stainless steel:** To remove smear marks, wipe the steel over with olive oil and a dab of pure white vinegar. Buff to shine.

- **Cobwebs:** To deter cobweb growth, mix 250 ml (8½ fl oz/1 cup) of cooking oil with the juice of three lemons in a spray bottle and spray on problem areas.

- **Glassware:** Mix 1 tablespoon of bicarbonate of soda (baking soda) with 1 teaspoon of water to create a thick paste and apply to glassware with a cloth. Wash as normal in hot water, then polish.

- **Kettle:** Put half a lemon in a kettle full of water and bring it to the boil. Repeat three times. Allow the kettle to cool, then dispose of the lemon and water.

- **Mirrors:** Apply lemonade (lemon soda) to a clean cloth, wipe over the mirror and polish with a soft flannel.

- **Whiten white clothes:** In a bucket, add 2 sliced lemons to 4 litres (135 fl oz/16 cups) of hot water and soak clothing for 10 minutes.

- **Wicker baskets:** Hose down outside and leave in the sun to dry out. Good as new!

SIMPLE STAIN REMOVERS

Tackle just about any stain with these home remedies. Apply directly to problem areas before washing as normal.

Grass: Dab a dash of diluted white vinegar onto the stain before washing.

Red wine: Saturate the stain with soda water (club soda) and blot it with a dry towel until the stain fades, then wash as normal.

Grease: Make a paste of bicarbonate of soda (baking soda) and water, paint onto the stain and watch the bicarb draw the stain out.

Blood: Soak the stained item in cold water then rub with a bar of soap, lathering gently before washing. Ensure the stain is removed before drying the article to avoid heat-setting the stain.

Oil: Rub the stain with white chalk and let it absorb before brushing the residue away. Repeat if necessary and wash the item as normal.

Coffee: Sprinkle some bicarbonate of soda (baking soda) on a cold wet cloth and gently massage it into the stain. Wash as normal.

Deodorant: Crush 3–4 aspirin tablets and combine with water to make a paste. Apply the paste to the stain and let it sit for a few hours before washing as normal.

Sweat: Rub half a cut lemon directly onto the sweat stains and wash as normal.

Lipstick: Blot with a baby wipe; wash as normal.

Ink: Soak the stained item overnight in a bowl filled with 2 parts milk and 1 part vinegar. Hang to dry then wash as normal.

Makeup: Use shaving cream to cut through the oil component of both liquid and cream makeup. Blot with a clean cloth to lift the stain then wash as normal.

FRESHEN UP YOUR BEDROOM

My bedroom is my sanctuary and a place in our home that I love to spend time. After months of being closed up for the winter, it is in desperate need of a refresh by spring. Although our bedroom is very calm and relaxing with only grey and white tones used in the decor, in spring, I like to mix it up a little with a fresh makeover.

A close girlfriend of mine, who owns a Melbourne-based business, sources her amazing hand-printed textiles in India. As much as I love my grey and white, spring calls for change so I find myself obsessing over her pale green, block-printed bed linen.

Mixing and matching patterns can be fun and interesting. The end result doesn't need to look messy if you make sure the main items, such as blankets, quilt covers and decorative throws, stay uniform. I'm not suggesting you change everything, but a fresh set of sheets that are a little different to what you had in winter will put a smile on your face and make you want to take an afternoon nap in the sun. Pops of colour here and there to break the monotony is exactly what a spring revamp is all about.

QUICK TIPS TO BRIGHTEN UP THE BEDROOM

◈ Always wash new bed linen before you use it.

◈ Iron your pillowcases and top sheet for extra crispness.

◈ Add plants to your room to give it an instant lift; try something simple like potted orchids in fresh moss.

◈ Go through the magazines and books next to your bed and give away anything you've read. It's time to get rid of that bedside table clutter.

◈ New spring pyjamas will make you feel more excited about heading to bed.

◈ Put a floral-scented candle in the bedroom to usher in spring.

◈ Give everything a good clean and vacuum, especially behind and under your bed. While you're at it, clean all the windows and mirrors, too. There is nothing better than when it all sparkles.

THE GUEST ROOM

❝ While you're in the mood for spring cleaning, why not rejuvenate your guest room? There are small touches you can add that will make your guests feel right at home.

When organising this space, I always assume my guest has forgotten things. I make sure I have it all available so they don't have to ask: plenty of towels, a selection of beautiful hand creams and soap, a comfortable dressing gown, bed socks and an extra throw for the bed to keep my guest cosy.

For the bedside table, you must include a carafe of water and a drinking glass, a stack of new magazines and a pretty posy of flowers. Make sure there is plenty of wardrobe space and extra coathangers for them to hang clothes and put away their luggage. If you have young kids or early risers, a sleeping mask and earplugs will be much appreciated by your guests.

HOW TO FOLD A FITTED SHEET

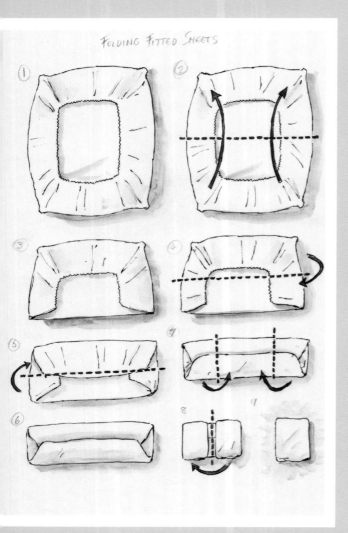

FOLDING FITTED SHEETS

1. Hold the sheet lengthways with the elastic facing you.

2. Fold the sheet in half widthways, with the elastic on the inside.

3. Tuck the corners into each other so the elastic now faces upwards.

4. Fold the top down to the middle of the sheet.

5. Fold the bottom up just past the midway point.

6. Make sure the sheet creates a neat rectangle.

7. Fold in the sides of the sheet so they meet in the middle.

8. Fold the right over the left side to create a neatly folded rectangle.

9. Now you are ready to store the sheet away.

BED LINEN TIPS AND TRICKS

◆ After you wash your linen, iron it just before it's fully dry. It makes the job so much easier.

◆ Spray your sheets with starch or linen spray to get that hotel look and feel.

◆ Iron your sheets on high and don't skip the pillowcases as they are the first thing you see when looking at a bed.

◆ In a hurry? When ironing, focus mostly on your pillowcases and the top quarter of your bed linen. They are the only parts visible when the bed is made. Sure, it's cheating, but who is ever going to know?

◆ Store your sheet sets inside their matching pillowcase, it makes it much easier to keep all the pieces together, and it stores neatly in your closet.

HOMEMADE LINEN WATER

Making your own linen water is an easy way to bring your favourite scent into the bedroom. I love to use lemon and rose oil.

What you'll need

30 drops (approx. ½ teaspoon) essential oil of your choice

90 ml (3 fl oz) vodka

375 ml (12½ fl oz/1½ cups) distilled water

—

MAKES APPROX. 500 ML (17 FL OZ/2 CUPS)

Mix the essential oil and vodka in a glass.

Add the distilled water and funnel the liquid into a spray bottle.

Shake the spray bottle before each use and keep it in a cool, dry place for up to six months.

SUM

MER

A SUMMER STATE OF MIND

" Oh summer ... those long days and warm nights. It's that delicious time of year when you can come home from work and enjoy a drink outside. The sun is shining, warm breezes blow in your hair and you can feel the lush grass between your toes. It's a season of feasting on stone fruit and enjoying special evenings with friends where anything seems possible. The floaty dresses come out and the kitchen bench is transformed into a farmers' market display with all the incredible produce available.

I love feeling the sun's warmth and hearing the birds chirping away. This is the time of year when being outside, watering the garden with a gin and tonic in hand, is total bliss. It just never lasts long enough.

ROSES

 When it comes to summer flowers, it's all about roses for me, particularly the pale pink, tangerine orange and watermelon tones. There is nothing I love more than walking into my local florist and seeing the new season's roses – the scent and colours are just fantastic.

A SUMMER ROMANCE

My absolute favourite roses are the David Austin range. There are some unusual varieties and some are almost the size of cabbages. They can also be a little ramshackle, but their imperfections just make me love them even more. It was these blooms that inspired me to create a rose-themed table for a girls' afternoon tea, where the flower is the hero on the table, and the inspiration for the colours and food.

I had been looking for a reason to use our barn doors as a backdrop for an informal gathering and when I saw how these light pink roses contrasted with the dark grey of the barn doors, I knew this was the perfect spot for an afternoon tea. I spent an idyllic morning baking and creating a rose-based cocktail before laying the table with everything I needed to make this stunning outdoor setting. From the rose flavouring of the sweets and drinks, to the colour combination of pink plates, rose-gold cutlery and peach-coloured vases, everything certainly came up roses.

Too often we only entertain at lunch or dinner, but why not mix it up? An afternoon tea is a far less formal way of entertaining. Plus, it gives us an excuse to focus solely on sweet treats, as naughty as they are.

YOU CAN NEVER HAVE TOO MANY VASES

Vases play a big part in this setting. I chose simple, pink-toned vases to allow the blooms and petals to shine with no distraction from the stems. I also used upside-down vases as cake stands. Dig deep into the back of your cupboards for this type of styling. You will need every vase you can find. You need enough to pile and layer to create a strong, decadent look.

THE SEMI-NAKED CAKE

The star of my rose-themed afternoon tea is a layered teacake with scrapings of icing, all topped with a handful of fresh rose heads. This style of dessert takes centre stage and is a real showstopper. The cake is actually three separate cakes layered on top of each other, with two layers of buttercream in between. Before you get started, have a look at my tips on how to make the perfect semi-naked cake on page 75.

5 eggs, at room temperature

450 g (1 lb/2 cups) caster (superfine) sugar

300 ml (10 fl oz) extra-virgin olive oil

300 g (10½ oz/1¼ cups) plain yoghurt

zest of ½ lemon

1½ tablespoons fresh lemon juice

450 g (1 lb/3 cups) self-raising flour

1 teaspoon cinnamon

pinch of salt

roses, to garnish (optional)

Buttercream

500 g (1 lb 2 oz/2 cups) unsalted butter, at room temperature

500 g (1 lb 2 oz/4 cups) icing (confectioners') sugar

125 ml (4½ fl oz/½ cup) lukewarm full cream (whole) milk

2 tablespoons vanilla extract

—

MAKES THREE 20 CM (8 IN) ROUND CAKES

Preheat the oven to 180°C (350°F).

Grease the base and sides of three 20 × 5 cm (8 × 2 in) round cake tins. Line each tin with baking paper.

Cream the eggs and sugar in a large bowl using an electric mixer. Gradually add the olive oil until emulsified, then add the yoghurt, lemon zest and juice and beat for 30 seconds until combined. Sift the self-raising flour, cinnamon and salt into the bowl and gently fold in using a metal spoon.

Pour the batter into the prepared cake tins and bake for 45 minutes, or until a skewer inserted in the centre comes out clean. Allow the cakes to cool a little before turning them onto wire racks to cool completely.

To prepare the buttercream, place the butter in a mixing bowl and, using a hand-held electric beater, mix until soft and pale. Gradually add the icing sugar and continue beating well for 5 minutes. Add the milk (you don't have to use it all) and the vanilla extract and mix to a smooth consistency.

Place the first cake layer, upside down, on a serving plate. Make sure the bottom is completely flat or you will have a wobbly cake (see the notes on page 75).

Spread about 1 cup of buttercream on top of the first layer, taking it just past the edges of the first cake. Carefully place the second cake upside down on top of the first cake and repeat the process.

Once you have placed the last cake, spread buttercream on top. Then, using a palette knife or spatula, lightly spread the remaining icing around the outside of the cake, starting from the top and moving down the sides, leaving some of the cake exposed.

Chill the cake in the fridge for 1 hour to set the icing before serving. Garnish with roses, if desired.

TIPS FOR MAKING THE PERFECT SEMI-NAKED CAKE

❖ It's all about the planning. Semi-naked cakes need to be as fresh as possible as they don't have a thick layer of icing to maintain their moisture.

❖ Grease your pans as well as you can so the cake can be easily removed from the tin and won't lose its shape. Imperfections can't be hidden in a cake like this.

❖ Allow time for the cakes to cool before adding icing and stacking them.

❖ If you are worried about your cakes drying out, brush them with a simple sugar syrup (see page 99), or use rose liqueur for that added hit of flavour.

❖ A strong, thick buttercream filling is a must. You want your layers to sit comfortably on one another without filling oozing out the sides.

❖ For a nice flat finish, trim the top off each cake with a sharp knife to create a stable flat surface, and stack the cakes upside down.

❖ The sides of the cake are the heroes, so go as naked or as dressed as you like. I like an uneven smearing, to make the cake look a little rustic. Make sure you leave a good layer of icing on top for the decorations to sit on.

❖ If you want to create a two-tiered cake as shown on page 74, make two-and-a-half batches of the batter and buttercream recipes and use a 24 cm (9½ in) round cake tin for the bottom-tier cakes. Prepare the smaller and larger cakes as described in the recipe, then assemble your tiers once the cakes have chilled to ensure everything is stable.

ROSE COCKTAIL

Roses aren't just for decoration; the petals also happen to be delicious. Incorporating rose petals in this stunning cocktail shows off the flower's versatility. This is the perfect drink to serve your guests on arrival as it has that undeniable scent of rose, which I think we can all agree is one of the most pleasant smells in the world. Use giant round ice cube trays, so the cube becomes the hero of the cocktail. Serve the drink in a long-stemmed cocktail glass.

350 ml (12 fl oz) bottled water

1 handful of fresh rose petals

60 ml (2 fl oz) Lillet Rose

60 ml (2 fl oz) red grapefruit juice

30 ml (1 fl oz) gin

–

SERVES 1

Make some ice cubes by filling an ice cube tray almost to the top with the bottled water and freeze. Once frozen, place a rose petal on each ice cube, then pour a teaspoon of water over it and freeze again.

Fill a cocktail shaker with ice and pour in the Lillet Rose, grapefruit juice and gin.

Shake until well chilled and strain into the cocktail glass.

Drop in a flower petal ice cube and serve immediately.

ROSE TEA

What better way to while away a sunny summer's afternoon than by having a tea party. A beautiful garden tea party would not be complete without delicate rose-flavoured tea and sweets to match.

2 handfuls of fresh rose petals (4 if you want a stronger rose flavour; ask your local florist for untreated petals, or source them at an organic grocer)

honey, to taste (if you want a sweetener)

–

SERVES 2

Rinse the rose petals in a colander.

Place the petals in a saucepan and pour in 750 ml (25½ fl oz/3 cups) water. Boil for 5 minutes, then strain into teacups.

Add honey, to taste, for sweetness.

HOW TO DRY ROSES

Air drying is the easiest way to dry roses but you must do it before the buds open. Simply tie a bunch of roses at the stems and hang them upside down for 6–8 weeks in a cool, dry place. They will take a couple of weeks to dry. Check on them every few days; you want them dry to the touch. Dried flowers can be stored in a sealed container until ready to use.

What to do with dried roses

- Fill a sachet with dried petals to freshen up your linen press.
- Make potpourri.
- Sprinkle them in a bath.
- Make a fragrant tea.
- Sprinkle them inside a gift.
- Use them as a beautiful alternative to confetti at a wedding.
- Sprinkle a handful of petals in the fire before burning for a subtle rose scent.

EXTEND THE LIFE OF ROSES

❖ Cut rose stems on an angle so they soak up more water.

❖ Cut away excess foliage below the water line to keep the water clean.

❖ Dissolve 3 tablespoons sugar and 2 tablespoons white vinegar in 250 ml (8½ fl oz/1 cup) warm water. This provides the sweetness and nutrition roses need to thrive once cut.

66 Preserve
the feel of
summer.

HOW TO PRESS FLOWERS

What you'll need

cardboard

newspaper

tissue paper

flowers for pressing (I recommend violets, pansies, forget-me-nots or roses)

heavy book (a phone book works well)

large brick or rock

—

Cut out a piece of cardboard of a similar size to your book. Place a sheet of newspaper on top of the cardboard followed by a piece of tissue paper. All three sheets should be roughly the same size.

Place your flowers on the tissue paper, making sure they don't touch each other or hang over the side of the paper.

Cover the flowers with another piece of tissue paper, then newspaper, then cardboard.

If you want to press more flowers, you can repeat this process, one on top of the other, until all your flowers are prepared.

Once your stack is done, put your heavy book on top followed by the brick or stone.

Set aside for about 2 to 4 weeks.

TOMATOES

" I love tomato season. It spells summer – tomato plants are heavy with ripe fruit in all shapes and colours, ready to be harvested to enjoy fresh, to cook with or to preserve for the rest of the year. And how better to celebrate the season than with drinks, dishes and decorations based on this versatile fruit?

A GREEN THUMB'S BIRTHDAY

 The ever-changing landscape and incredible vistas of the Victorian countryside were the perfect backdrop for this special birthday lunch for my mother. Anyone who walks around my mum's property will instantly recognise that she loves gardening. So, what theme do you go with for a green thumb's birthday? Tomatoes, of course.

Tomatoes just scream summer to me. Using different varieties of tomatoes as the table centrepiece, I layered, scattered and arranged them, mixing up the heights, colours and shapes. I stuck to a colour theme of red, green and white and I was able to bring in more of these tones and patterns with some red-and-white chequered tea towels disguised as napkins, ceramic plates emblazoned with a beautiful leaf pattern and, of course, the environment in which the table sat.

I placed packaged seeds next to the guests' place cards. They make great gifts – everyone gets to take home a packet of seeds for their own garden. This table had such great texture that I didn't want to hide it with a tablecloth. Instead, I kept it uncovered and filled the centre with terracotta pots full of tomato plants and herbs that could be picked and used as a garnish for the meals.

TERRIFIC TOMATOES

 There are so many tomato varieties out there, of all shapes, sizes and even colour. To make the most of them you need to be aware of how different varieties can be used in the kitchen, whether cooked, tossed in a salad or simply eaten on their own.

- **Heirloom tomatoes:** Best served simply in a salad or on toast with lashings of salt and pepper.

- **Cherry tomatoes:** The smallest and sweetest tomatoes. Great in salads, on their own, or roasted for their sweet taste. They also make a delicious and colourful garnish for a platter.

- **Black Russian:** Dramatic colour and a strong taste. Sandwiches never tasted so good.

- **Vine-ripened tomatoes:** Ideal for roasting or as a base for tomato soups, pasta sauces and juice.

- **Yellow cherry tomatoes:** The go-to tomato for salads and snacking.

TIPS FOR RIPENING TOMATOES

If you grow your own tomatoes, it's important to know how to get the best fruit from your plant. Once your tomatoes have started appearing and grown to full size, it's time to let them ripen. Do these things and you'll have lovely, ripe tomatoes ready for your kitchen.

◈ Reduce watering when your tomatoes are firm and have just a tinge of green.

◈ Cut back any excess or dead foliage to redirect the plant's energy into growing fruit.

◈ Pick off any small or excess fruit.

◈ Cover plants with netting while the fruit is ripening to protect it from birds and other animals.

◈ Check tomato plants daily for any pests, fungus or disease, and discard any diseased leaves.

◈ **TOP TIP:** If you pick your tomato before it is fully ripe, pop it in a paper bag with a banana, out of direct sunlight. It will ripen within a few days.

BLOODY MARY

A Bloody Mary is the perfect way to start off a summer lunch. It can be garnished with a variety of things and made as spicy as you like. Use a plain tall glass so that the beautiful colours of the tomato juice and garnish take pride of place. Have the drinks lined up on a tray, or make up a bar with all the ingredients at the ready – vodka, tomato juice, sauces, spices and garnishes to cater to each guest's taste. Adding leafy stalks of celery and wedges of lemon to your Bloody Mary is a fun way to style your drink, and a bar set-up is a great talking point for guests.

ice cubes

60 ml (2 fl oz/¼ cup) vodka

120 ml (4 fl oz) tomato juice

½ tablespoon lemon juice

1 splash worcestershire sauce

3 dashes Tabasco sauce

1 teaspoon horseradish paste

salt and freshly ground black pepper, to taste

celery stalk, to garnish

lemon wedge, to garnish

–

SERVES 1

Place 2–3 ice cubes in a tall glass.

Add all the ingredients except the celery stalk and lemon wedge to a chilled cocktail shaker and shake well, then strain into the glass.

Add a pinch of salt and freshly ground black pepper, to taste. Garnish with the celery and lemon wedge.

TOMATO & RICOTTA TARTS

375 g (13 oz) shortcrust pastry

200 g (7 oz) firm ricotta

20 g (¾ oz) finely grated parmesan

¼ cup mixed herbs such as basil or flat-leaf (Italian) parsley, coarsely chopped, plus extra leaves to garnish (optional)

zest of 1 lemon and juice of ½ lemon

1 egg, lightly beaten

salt and freshly ground black pepper

1 large, ripe oxheart tomato, cut into six wedges

200 g (7 oz) mixed cherry tomatoes, halved or quartered, depending on their size

75 ml (2½ fl oz) extra-virgin olive oil

1 tablespoon red-wine vinegar

–

MAKES 6 TARTS

Preheat the oven to 200°C (400°F) and grease six 10 cm (4 in) fluted tart tins with olive oil spray. Make sure you coat the entire tin. Line each tin with pastry and trim the edges.

Combine the ricotta, parmesan, herbs, lemon zest and half the beaten egg in a bowl. Season with salt and pepper and mix to combine. Divide the filling between the pastry-lined tins.

Brush the rim of the pastry lightly with the remaining egg then bake for 10–15 minutes, rotating occasionally, until golden brown.

Combine the tomatoes, olive oil, vinegar and lemon juice in a bowl. Season to taste. When the tarts are done, pile some tomato mixture on top and scatter with herbs, if using. Serve warm.

HOMEMADE TOMATO SAUCE

Everybody loves a gutsy tomato sauce to have with their barbecue or pie, and this one is so delicious. Package it up in a jar for a special gift.

2 tablespoons olive oil

1 small onion, peeled and chopped

2 garlic cloves, crushed

300 g (10½ oz) tinned peeled tomatoes, drained

2 tablespoons tomato paste

1 tablespoon soft brown sugar

1 tablespoon worcestershire sauce

1 tablespoon sweet chilli sauce

2 tablespoons white-wine vinegar

1 tablespoon dijon mustard

1 squeeze of lemon

–

MAKES 450 ML (15 FL OZ)

Heat the oil in a saucepan over a low heat and fry the onion for 5 minutes until softened slightly.

Add all the other ingredients and bring to the boil.

Squeeze in some lemon juice, reduce the heat to medium and cook for 5 minutes, stirring occasionally, until the sauce has thickened slightly. Set it aside to cool.

Blend the sauce in a blender until smooth.

Store in an airtight container in the refrigerator for up to 2 weeks.

PERUVIAN BARBECUE

❝❝ I love to travel and one of my favourite countries is the incredible Peru. I was blown away by all the colour used in the textiles and rugs. I really couldn't help myself and just had to bring a few bits and pieces home, which I've used here to style a Peruvian barbecue.

WELCOME
TO PERU

" A barbecue is a casual affair and I was lucky enough to create this setting for a friend in her outdoor garden space. A look like this is so easy to achieve; you can add as much or as little as your heart desires. I created layers of colour by covering the stone floor with vibrant, patterned rugs, using bright fun fabric for the table and scattering cushions about. Dining in this style invites your guests to sit down and relax.

The long dining table was the perfect set-up for a food buffet and it quickly became the focal area of the space when I added masses of brightly coloured ranunculus flowers in simple tins. It's always important to have depth and height on a table, which I created by layering the food on wooden boxes and platforms.

Buffet-style food is perfect for low-maintenance entertaining – you can set things up and fill the table with everything you need before the party starts. Just lay out the plates, cutlery, serviettes and plenty of serving cutlery along with your condiments and dressings, then, once the food is ready, you're free to just enjoy yourself.

66 For a Peruvian-themed party one *must* start the night with a Pisco Sour. It is the traditional drink of Peru, with a strong but delicious kick of pisco, a type of brandy. This drink is so popular in Peru that it has its own day of celebration on the first weekend in February. I love to introduce my friends to a new tipple when I have a themed party – it's a great conversation starter. Have a drinks cart set up ready to go, with plenty of ice and glasses, so your guests can help themselves on arrival.

PISCO SOUR

60 ml (2 fl oz/¼ cup) pisco (I prefer Pisco Barsol Quebranta but any brand will do)

30 ml (1 fl oz) fresh lime juice

15 ml (½ fl oz) sugar syrup (see method)

1 fresh egg white

dash of Angostura bitters

lime wedge, to garnish

mint sprig, to garnish

–

SERVES 1

If you're making your own sugar syrup, bring 230 g (8 oz/1 cup) caster (superfine) sugar and 250 ml (8½ fl oz/1 cup) water to the boil in a small saucepan over a low heat. Stir until the sugar has dissolved, then remove from the heat and allow to cool. Store excess syrup in a sealed container in the refrigerator.

Put all the ingredients except the bitters and lime wedge into a cocktail shaker and fill it with ice.

Shake vigorously then strain into a highball or martini glass.

Garnish with a lime wedge and mint sprig and 3 drops of Angostura bitters, which will settle in the foam of the cocktail.

Using a straw, swirl the bitters into a pattern.

PERUVIAN FEAST

 I love Peruvian food. The flavours, spices and textural combinations are truly delicious. There was no shortage of delicacies to choose from when I travelled through this amazing country. The flavours of Peru come from a variety of influences – African, Arab, European and Asian – with a clear focus on eating what is in season and locally grown, so you can only imagine the variety of cooking styles and unique dishes.

AVOCADO, TOMATO & CHEESE SALAD

4 rashers (slices) bacon

2 avocados, peeled, pitted and cut into 2 cm (¾ in) cubes

2 medium-sized tomatoes, peeled, seeded and cut into 2 cm (¾ in) cubes

450 g (1 lb) fresh cheese (queso fresco, fresh mozzarella or other fresh, soft cheese) or cheddar cheese, cut into cubes

salt and freshly ground black pepper, to taste

3 tablespoons extra-virgin olive oil

—

SERVES 4

Pan-fry the bacon over a medium–high heat. Allow it to cool, then tear into irregular strips.

In a large bowl, combine the avocado, tomato, cheese and bacon.

Season to taste with salt and pepper.

Add the olive oil and toss gently before serving.

QUINOA, AVOCADO & SWEET CORN SALAD

75 g (2¾ oz) uncooked quinoa

135 g (5 oz/⅔ cup) sweet corn kernels (fresh or frozen)

1 tablespoon extra-virgin olive oil

75 g (2¾ oz) cherry tomatoes, quartered

handful of coriander (cilantro) leaves, roughly chopped

2 spring onions (scallions), finely sliced

finely grated zest and juice of 1 lime

½ long red chilli, finely chopped

salt and freshly ground black pepper

1 ripe but firm avocado, halved and stoned

30 g (1 oz/¼ cup) mixed nuts (brazil nuts, almonds, hazelnuts, pecans and walnuts)

—

SERVES 4–6

Cook the quinoa according to the packet instructions. Meanwhile, heat the sweet corn in a dry frying pan over a medium-high heat. Cook for 5–6 minutes, turning every now and then, until lightly toasted. Set aside.

Rinse the cooked quinoa under cold water and drain to remove excess water. Tip the quinoa into a bowl and toss in the olive oil, sweet corn, tomatoes, coriander, spring onion, lime zest and chilli. Season with black pepper, to taste.

Slice the avocado and toss it with the lime juice, then add it to the salad with the nuts. Toss gently before serving.

POLLO A LA BRASA (GRILLED CHICKEN)

80 ml (2½ fl oz /⅓ cup) soy sauce

2 tablespoons fresh lime juice

5 garlic cloves

2 teaspoons ground cumin

1 teaspoon paprika

½ teaspoon dried oregano

½ teaspoon freshly ground black pepper

1 tablespoon vegetable oil

1 × 1.5 kg (3 lb 5 oz) whole chicken, quartered

1 lime, quartered, to garnish

–

SERVES 4

To make the marinade, put the soy sauce, lime juice, garlic cloves, cumin, paprika, oregano, pepper and oil in a blender and whiz until combined.

Put the chicken in a large zip-lock bag and pour in the marinade. Seal the bag and marinate in the fridge for 8–24 hours. Turn the bag occasionally to ensure even marinating.

Heat a barbecue or chargrill pan to medium–high and oil the grill rack (if using a barbecue).

Place the chicken on the grill rack or in the pan and chargrill, turning once until cooked through (approximately 30–35 minutes).

Garnish with lime wedges.

THYME & CRISPY SHALLOT POTATOES

3 tablespoons unsalted butter, melted

3 tablespoons extra-virgin olive oil

1.8 kg (4 lb) russet potatoes, peeled

4 shallots, thickly sliced lengthways

salt

1 teaspoon red chilli flakes

8 thyme sprigs, chopped

–

SERVES 4

Preheat the oven to 190°C (375°F).

In a small bowl, combine the butter and oil, and use it to grease the bottom of a round, 23 cm (9 in) baking dish.

Using a sharp knife or mandoline, slice the potatoes crossways very thinly.

Arrange the potato slices vertically in the baking dish, wedging shallot slices throughout. Sprinkle with the salt and chilli flakes and brush with the remaining butter mixture.

Bake for 75 minutes.

Add the thyme to the potatoes and continue to bake for another 35 minutes, until the potatoes are cooked through and crispy on top.

GRILLED LAMB CHOPS WITH HERBS & SPICES

125 ml (4 fl oz/½ cup) extra-virgin olive oil, plus 2 tablespoons for frying

3–4 garlic cloves, sliced

½ brown onion, finely chopped

2 rosemary sprigs

10 thyme sprigs

½ teaspoon ground cumin

½ teaspoon ground cardamom

1 pinch cayenne pepper, or to taste

1 teaspoon balsamic vinegar

8–12 bone-in lamb chops, 2½–3 cm (1–1½ in) thick

coarse salt and freshly ground black pepper, to taste

mint or flat-leaf (Italian) parsley, to garnish

–

SERVES 4

In a small frying pan, heat the 2 tablespoons of olive oil over a medium heat.

Sauté the garlic and onion until the garlic is golden brown and the onion is tender. Remove from the heat and immediately transfer the garlic and onion into a food processor, along with the herbs and spices. Pulse for 30 seconds to 1 minute. Add the olive oil and balsamic vinegar and continue to pulse to a purée.

Lay the lamb chops in a shallow dish. Pour the marinade over and massage it into the meat.

Cover the chops and refrigerate for 2 hours, turning them occasionally to ensure they marinate evenly. Remove the lamb from the refrigerator and rest (still in the marinade) for 25 minutes at room temperature.

Preheat your barbecue or chargrill pan to high.

Place the lamb chops on the centre of the grill rack or pan, and chargrill. Sear for 2–3 minutes, then flip and cook the other side for 3 minutes (for medium-rare) or 4 minutes (for medium). Baste the lamb with the marinade while it's cooking to keep the meat juicy.

Take the lamb off the heat, season to taste with salt and pepper and let it rest for 3–5 minutes.

Garnish with mint or flat leaf parsley and serve with Thyme and crispy shallot potatoes (page 104) and Peruvian green sauce (see opposite page).

PERUVIAN GREEN SAUCE

Best served with lamb or chicken.

1–2 medium-sized fresh jalapeños, seeds and membranes removed

1 tablespoon aji amarillo paste (available at specialty food stores or online; you can substitute with chilli paste if required)

45 g (1½ oz/1¼ cups) fresh coriander (cilantro) leaves and stems

15 g (½ oz/¼ cup) fresh basil leaves

2 tablespoons grated parmesan cheese

1 tablespoon finely chopped fresh ginger

1 teaspoon honey

1 medium garlic clove

1 tablespoon sunflower or canola oil

2 tablespoons fresh lime juice

125 g (4½ oz/½ cup) mayonnaise

salt and freshly ground black pepper

—

MAKES 250 ML (8½ FL OZ) (APPROX)

Combine all the ingredients except the mayonnaise in a blender and blend on high speed until a smooth paste forms.

Add the mayonnaise and blend until combined.

Season with salt and pepper, to taste.

Leftover sauce can be stored in the refrigerator, in an airtight container or jar with a tight-fitting lid, for up to 1 week.

OUTDOORS

" The sun is shining and the days are longer, so let's get outside and enjoy it! There is nothing better than spending a summer's day in the garden or a nearby park. Feel the warm breeze on your skin, close your eyes and let your mind wander …

SUMMER SUNSHINE

66 Bringing this gorgeous daybed outside and filling it with cushions is my idea of heaven. I layered tones of blue, turquoise and white to create a feeling of serenity and coolness on a hot summer's day. My gorgeous friend had these cushions block-printed in India. I love that by keeping the colours the same, but mixing and matching the patterns, you can create a pretty, layered effect. Layering a couple of different rugs over one another brings the whole look together.

Of course, this look can be simplified. Even if it's just a new tablecloth on an outside table, some matching seat cushions and a newly potted plant – you will still get that hit of summer colour. Maybe buy a new jug and glasses in a fun colour to complete your fresh summer look. We don't all have big gardens; you might only have a small balcony, but that doesn't mean you can't create something special, just for you. There is always a favourite corner that has beautiful morning or afternoon sunlight inviting you to curl up and soak up some of those warming rays.

Before you start styling, think about how you will use your sunny spot. Is it a reading nook or a sunbaking spot? A place for a quiet cup of tea or to catch up with friends? Bring colour in with cushions and throws, and don't be scared to go a little crazy with it; this is the season and space to let loose.

Time to mix up a batch of cocktails and call your friends over? First, make sure you have tables to rest a drink on and that your space is as comfortable as possible, with some extra throws so you won't need anything else once you are outside. If it's just you, all you need to do is find your favourite book, grab something to drink and head outside to enjoy your special summer space. But first, make sure it's as practical as possible. The last thing you want is to have to move everything in and out every day. Have a big basket handy that you can pile everything back into, or a storage container you can hide under a chair.

When the sun starts setting, create a romantic mood with large lanterns of varying heights and be sure to surround yourself with some summer flowers. Hydrangeas really give that summer feel; they are robust, hearty and work well en masse in large pots or vases.

GET CLEANING WHILE THE SUN SHINES

After a cold, wet winter, there is nothing better than swinging open the back doors and windows and entertaining outside again. That probably means you need to check how your outdoor furniture, decking and garden are looking. After a long winter, furniture often needs to be repainted, the decking might need to be re-stained, cushions might need a scrub down and the brickwork may have grown moss. Wait for that perfect sunny day, then jump into jobs like checking the gutters, removing cobwebs, cleaning your outdoor umbrella and giving your back step a real going-over. Maybe it's time to invest in some new outdoor cushions or to pot some colourful flowers and give your terracotta pots a good clean. Then it's time to enjoy the sun!

Outdoor cleaning

Cushions: Mix ½ tablespoon dishwashing detergent and 1 tablespoon white vinegar with 500 ml (17 fl oz/2 cups) lukewarm water in a spray bottle. Give it a good shake and spray your cushions with the mixture. Let them sit for 10–20 minutes, hose them off, then leave them to dry in the sun. Use a little elbow grease for the edges and crevices and give them a good scrub.

Outdoor tiles: You don't need soaps, detergents, powders or chemical cleaners of any kind to clean your outdoor tiles. Simply give them a good sweep then mop with a few drops of vinegar in a bucket of warm water. Don't use too much water on the mop as it will push the dirt into the grout.

Barbecue: Scrape away all the grit from the plates and grills with a wire scrubbing brush, making sure you scrape both sides. Soak all your barbecue plates and grills in hot soapy water for at least 30 minutes – the hotter the better; you want to get rid of all the grease. While they are drying, clean the rest of the barbecue with hot soapy water and a scourer. Once the plates and grills have dried, spray them with cooking spray and put them back in the barbecue. Swap your drip trays over every few times you barbecue.

Wooden furniture: Wipe down all pieces of furniture with hot, soapy water (sugar soap or detergent works well). Use a scrubbing brush for tougher stains, then give it all a good spray with the hose and leave it to dry. This job is best done at the start of summer so it's freshly cleaned and ready for outdoor entertaining.

AUT

UMN

AUTUMN IS THE TIME FOR CHANGE

 After a long, hot summer, nothing is better than bright, beautiful days and cool nights. Autumn brings beautiful changes in nature – the leaves turn the most glorious colours, from bright yellow through to copper; burnt orange to red, and I'm inspired to entertain my friends with food that matches these tones. In autumn, my tastebuds tingle at the thought of roast pumpkin (winter squash), parsnip and sweet potato. I am also a big believer in adjusting your home and decor to suit the seasons. In autumn, I love changing the fragrant smell of my candles to a warmer, more masculine, aroma, and, in the evening, I enjoy creating a soft, amber glow with the lamps in the house.

DARLING DAHLIAS

"" At this time of year, I simply can't go past the beautiful dahlia, which starts to flower around late summer/early autumn. There are so many varieties and colours, it's impossible to choose a favourite; from almost-black to the bi-colour varieties, they are just stunning. Dahlia flowers will last about a week in a vase, so their lifespan isn't long, but boy, do they look exquisite when they are in full bloom.

TEA AMONG
THE DAHLIAS

 A sweet outdoor afternoon tea was the perfect excuse for me to decorate with bunches and bunches of dahlias. Floral foam (this can be found at florists) is a really effective way to show off these beautiful flowers and make a floral centrepiece that has real wow factor. Some of my favourite tones are luscious pink, orange and red, and I love clumping them together to make a brilliant display of blooms. Dahlias just shine when displayed en masse.

HOW TO MAKE
A DAHLIA
BLOCK

What you'll need

floral foam (available
at florists. Use bricks,
balls or whatever
shape you like)

secateurs

dahlias

lazy susan (optional)

tray or plate

spray bottle full
of water

—

Soak the floral foam in water for at least 30 minutes so your flowers stay hydrated. Use as many blocks as you like to create your table centrepiece.

Cut each flower stem close to the head, leaving just enough stem to poke into the foam.

Keep turning your block and poking in dahlias until it is evenly covered in flower heads. A lazy susan is perfect for this job!

When your block is finished, put it on a tray or plate so the water doesn't wet your table or tablecloth.

Spray your flowers with water to keep them fresh.

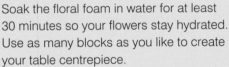

DAHLIA FACTS AND TIPS

◈ There are more than 30 varieties of dahlias and a vast array of colours.

◈ They are native to Mexico.

◈ Flower width can range from 5 cm (2 in) to 20 cm (8 in). The larger ones are nicknamed 'dinner-plate dahlias'.

◈ Dahlias tend to turn vase water brown quite quickly, so it's important to trim excess leaves off the stems so they aren't submerged. It's also a good idea to trim the stems and change the water every 2–3 days.

◈ Use secateurs or a sharp knife to cut dahlias (household scissors can bruise their stems), then immediately put them in a bucket of cool water to prevent wilting.

◈ Dahlias have a vase life of about 1 week and thrive out of direct sunlight.

DECORATING
WITH DAHLIAS

66 One of the things I love about dahlias is the huge variety of colours and shapes available.

Dahlias are also inexpensive, so you can buy multiple bunches to bulk out an arrangement. I tend to stick to one colour palette and mix up the shapes and sizes of blooms. I don't mix varieties together either as I think you achieve a stronger result with a uniform look.

Having colour in your home in autumn is such a treat, so I do go overboard. The coffee table literally groans under the weight of the different vases, but it looks fantastic. Use a variety of different-sized vases to layer up and mix in between your lanterns, books and other personal items. You really will get lots of 'oohs' and 'ahs' when your friends come over.

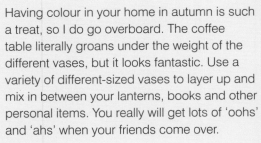

VEGETABLES

" No matter if you are after hearty soups and stews, colourful salads with leafy greens or roast root vegetables, Mother Nature provides options aplenty in autumn. The deep, dark greens, purples, bright oranges and glorious patterns and textures of autumn vegetables are a sight to behold in themselves and can take pride of place in your styling, not just your cooking!

PUMPKIN TABLE

 Using seasonal vegetables as a centrepiece instead of flowers is a quirky and unexpected way to style an outdoor table and will really impress your guests. I love mixing it up and getting creative with everyday objects, and this table is a perfect example. There is a huge variety of root vegetables here – pumpkins (winter squash), gourds, sweet potatoes, parsnips and potatoes, along with kale and artichokes. All of these vegetables are coming into season and have that beautiful autumnal colour palette, which just excites my styling eye so much.

To create this centrepiece, I started with pumpkins of varying heights, stacked across the table in a style that almost creates a hedge. From there I filled the gaps with softer bunches of cabbages, parsnips, artichokes and smaller, crazy-looking gourds. You really can't go wrong creating a table like this; there are no rules for how the vegetables should be placed. And rest assured, none of it will be wasted afterwards. Roast vegetable soup anyone?

I covered the table with hessian (burlap) to give it a lovely rustic feel. Hessian isn't often used as a tablecloth due to its roughness, but it's inexpensive and readily available, so why not experiment with it? You don't need to hem it or worry about creasing either; it's all about simplicity and creating a neutral base that allows the colours of the vegetables to sing.

Don't just think about what will be on the table though – think about where you set it up. Pick a beautiful, visually exciting spot outside in the autumn sun. I love this part of my parents' garden. It's got an incredible view overlooking the trees and rolling hills, and it's so green and lush. At this time of year, the leaves are at their most colourful and perfectly match what is on the table.

THE PERFECT ROAST VEGETABLES

ROASTING TIMES FOR VEGETABLES

Cooking times are for an oven pre-heated to 220°C (430°F).

- **Root vegetables** (beetroot [beets], potatoes, carrots): 30–45 minutes.

- **Brassicas/crucifers** (broccoli, cauliflower, brussels sprouts): 15–25 minutes.

- **Soft vegetables** (zucchini [courgette], summer squash, capsicum [bell peppers]): 10–20 minutes.

- **Thin vegetables** (asparagus, green beans): 10–20 minutes.

- **Onions**: 30 minutes (45 minutes if you like them crispy).

Autumn always inspires me to make a delicious side of vegetables to be enjoyed by the whole family, and with so many gorgeous colours and flavours in season, there's no limit to what you can mix up and roast.

The golden rule when roasting vegetables is to cut all your veggies to the same, uniform size. There is nothing more annoying than having varying degrees of texture and edibility because one potato is cut smaller than the others. Don't be scared of dousing the veggies in olive oil either; you want them well-coated so they absorb a sprinkling of salt and a handful of herbs. Give your veggies a good toss and always make sure they have plenty of room in the tray – crowding will create a steamy situation. You want them crunchy and roasted, not soggy and steamed. Once the seasoning is taken care of, simply pop them in the oven until you see some lovely, golden toasted colour, and enjoy! Don't be afraid to season your veggies again with lashings of salt and pepper, and mix through a good handful of fresh herbs when they come out of the oven.

Roasted root vegetable salad

1 celeriac

1 lemon, cut into wedges

8–10 Dutch carrots, trimmed and washed

2 parsnips, peeled and cut into wedges

1 red onion, cut into wedges

6–8 beetroots (beets), trimmed, peeled and cut into wedges

80 ml (2½ fl oz/⅓ cup) olive oil, plus 2 extra tablespoons

2 tablespoons balsamic vinegar

1 garlic clove, crushed

1 teaspoon brown sugar

100 g (3½ oz/2 cups) baby spinach leaves

—

SERVES 4

Preheat the oven to 200°C (400°F).

Using a sharp knife, remove the skin from the celeriac and cut it into wedges. Put the celeriac in a bowl of water with the lemon wedges (this prevents it from browning) while you prepare the remaining vegetables.

Place the carrots, parsnips, red onion and beetroot in a large baking tray. Drain and pat dry the celeriac and add it to the tray. Drizzle with the 2 tablespoons of olive oil and toss the vegetables until well coated.

Bake for 30 minutes, checking halfway through to see if the vegetables are browning evenly. Turn if necessary.

Meanwhile, in a small bowl, whisk together the olive oil, balsamic vinegar, garlic and brown sugar, and set aside.

When the vegetables are done, remove them from the oven and allow to cool slightly.

In a large salad bowl, toss the warm roasted vegetables with the baby spinach leaves, then drizzle over the dressing. Ready to serve!

KALE CAESAR SALAD

300 g (10½ oz) fresh kale, chopped

300 g (10½ oz) cos (romaine) lettuce, chopped

60 g (2 oz/2 cups) croutons

50 g (1¾ oz/½ cup) parmesan cheese, grated

Lime dressing

125 g (4½ oz/½ cup) plain Greek yoghurt

3–4 tablespoons fresh lime juice

1 tablespoon extra-virgin olive oil

1–2 teaspoons anchovy paste, to taste

2 teaspoons worcestershire sauce

1 garlic clove, pressed or finely minced

1 teaspoon dijon mustard

pinch of sea salt

pinch of freshly ground black pepper

—

SERVES 4–6

Place the kale, lettuce, croutons and parmesan in a large bowl.

To make the dressing, whisk together all ingredients in a small mixing bowl until smooth and combined. Pour it over the salad and toss until combined.

Serve immediately.

AUTUMN ARTICHOKE DIP

An autumn favourite on my vegetable-inspired table is hot artichoke dip. It's a little bit naughty, but is a total crowd-pleaser and deliciously easy to make. This cheesy dip, served with crisp lavosh or some crunchy warm bread, is a simple snack that can be whipped up on the fly when guests turn up unexpectedly.

200 g (7 oz/2 cups) grated parmesan cheese

280 g (10 oz) frozen chopped spinach, thawed and drained of excess liquid

400 g (14 oz) tinned artichoke hearts, drained and chopped

170 ml (5½ fl oz/⅔ cup) sour cream

250 g (9 oz/1 cup) cream cheese

90 g (3 oz/⅓ cup) mayonnaise

2 garlic cloves, crushed

—

SERVES 8–10

Preheat the oven to 190°C (375°F).

Mix the parmesan cheese, spinach and artichoke hearts together in an 8 cm (3¼ in) pie or flan dish.

Place the remaining ingredients in another bowl and whisk to combine, then pour over the spinach mixture.

Bake for 20–30 minutes.

Serve with crackers or toasted bread.

LEAVES

" Autumn is a stunning time of year that seems to go by much too fast. After a hot summer, there is nothing more beautiful than seeing the leaves change from green to red, then orange to yellow. It is the perfect time to get creative with an autumnal colour palette to celebrate the season.

AUTUMNAL
CRUNCH

 The light on an autumn day plays a big part in how our gardens and homes look at this time of year, and walking through a bed of autumn leaves, hearing them crunch underneath you, one can't help but feel inspired by and connected to nature.

I set this table under romantic fallen leaves in the golden light of an autumn afternoon. When confronted with a leaf-littered dining table, most people would sweep everything away and clear the area of leaves, but I wanted to celebrate them; to show them off and work with nature, not against it. The more leaves, the better, I say! Embrace the colourful mess of autumn and use the leaves as inspiration. To add more layers, I brought in bundles of branches in different colours to give the dining space even more textural, autumnal crunch.

I complemented my rustic tablecloth of leaves with freshly cut wooden trunks as placemats and put my plates and cutlery on top. I also brought in some rosehip branches to match the red leaves that were scattered throughout. The colours speak for themselves.

With any theme, I like to carry it through from tabletop to menu. Playing around in the autumn leaves, I couldn't help but gravitate towards dolmades, a beautiful Greek finger food that matches perfectly with a glass of your favourite wine. These leaf-wrapped parcels of goodness are so easy to make, and again, reflect the autumn theme and the colours of nature.

I love to make food that creates a little 'ooh' and 'ah' when you serve it; it just makes going to the effort of styling a beautiful table so worthwhile. Your menu doesn't have to be elaborate. As long as you stay within a rustic, autumnal theme and use in-season produce, you can't go wrong.

GREEK DOLMADES

60 vine leaves (fresh or preserved), rinsed and drained

185 g (6½ oz) long-grain white rice

250 ml (8½ fl oz/1 cup) extra-virgin olive oil

2 medium brown onions, finely chopped

juice of 2 lemons

sea salt and freshly ground black pepper, to taste

2 tablespoons dill, chopped

15 g (½ oz/½ cup) flat-leaf (Italian) parsley, chopped

–

MAKES 50

If using preserved vine leaves, rinse them first and remove the stems, then leave them in a colander to drain. If using fresh vine leaves, wash them thoroughly, remove the stems and blanch them in boiling water. Remove the leaves with a slotted spoon and place them in a colander to cool completely. While waiting for the leaves to cool, rinse the uncooked rice under running water.

Heat a large saucepan over a medium heat. Add one-third of the olive oil and sauté the onions until translucent.

Add the rice and sauté for another minute. Pour in 500 ml (17 fl oz/2 cups) warm water and the juice of one lemon. Simmer for about 7 minutes, until the rice absorbs all the water and is parboiled. Season with salt and pepper and stir in the herbs. Remove from the stove and set aside to cool down for a while. This will be the filling for the dolmades.

Layer the bottom of a large pot with some vine leaves then start rolling the dolmades. Place one vine leaf (shiny side down) on a flat surface and add 1 teaspoon of the filling at the bottom (stem) end. Be careful not to overfill it as the rice will expand during cooking. Fold and roll the leaf up tightly so it looks like a little parcel, and place the stuffed vine leaves (fold side down) on the bottom of the pot. Keep going until all your dolmades are rolled, layering up tightly in the pot. Be careful not to leave any gaps between the dolmades to prevent them from cracking open when cooking.

Drizzle the dolmades with the rest of the olive oil and lemon juice, and season with salt and pepper. Place an inverted plate on top to hold the dolmades down while cooking and pour in enough water to cover them completely. Simmer over a low heat for about 30–40 minutes, until the water has been absorbed and only the dolmades and oil remain.

Remove from the heat. Remove the lid and plate, and let the dolmades cool for at least 30 minutes.

Serve this delicious Greek appetiser cold or at room temperature with a squeeze of lemon.

THE GIFT OF AUTUMN

 Take inspiration from the season and incorporate autumnal colour into your gift-giving as well. Grab some ordinary brown wrapping paper and a few autumn leaves, then paint the leaves and use them like stamps, pressing them against the paper to create incredible patterns. Leave it to dry and you'll have some beautiful wrapping paper. This is one of those fun autumn craft activities you can get into on a rainy day with the kids. We sometimes forget how beautiful nature is when we step inside our homes, but this is one way of bringing a little of autumn's magic indoors.

GET CREATIVE WITH AUTUMN LEAVES

◈ Collect autumn leaves of all shapes and sizes and glue them to A5 sheets of paper. Using double-sided tape or Blu Tack, simply attach them to a wall to create a grid-like display. Pin in rows of three, four or five. You want a mass of at least 20 leaf images.

◈ Find two glass vases of varying sizes. Sit the smaller vase inside the larger one and fill the gap between the two with a selection of autumn leaves.

◈ Got a plain table cloth? With a small roller and some paint, you can block-print your table cloth with an autumn leaf motif. Simply roll paint onto an autumn leaf and press it into the fabric. Once you're happy with the print, iron it to heat-set it. You'll only be able to spot-clean the tablecloth from now on though.

AROUND THE HOUSE

> ❝ The long summer days are over, and we are beginning to retreat indoors. This is a perfect time to tackle those long-neglected jobs around the house – organise your kitchen cupboards and pantry, sort out your laundry, and prepare your wardrobe and clothing for the cold weather ahead.

THE KITCHEN

" No doubt about it, the kitchen is the heart of my home. It's where all the action takes place, so of course I want it to be a beautiful space. Surrounding yourself with objects that are functional as well as beautiful will inspire you to cook with love and passion. I'm a firm believer that if you enjoy cooking a meal, the people you are serving it to will taste that love.

Making your kitchen look gorgeous and inviting all comes down to the details. Potted herbs next to your preparation area will inspire you to cook with them, while displaying your favourite crockery will inspire you to serve food on it. Don't let family heirlooms gather dust; use them, and keep them on display for all to see.

Create vignettes by grouping cutlery in jars, next to a selection of flavoured salts. If it's a little dark, bring a lamp to your bench and surround the base with collections of quirky utensils. Most importantly, have fun with it and turn your kitchen into a space you actually want to cook in.

DISPLAY YOUR COLLECTIONS IN CLUSTERS

" Let's face it, if you have more than three of something, you are starting a collection. It doesn't matter what you collect, anything can look creative en masse, particularly in a vase or under a glass dome.

Your local hardware store is a great place to find inexpensive bits and bobs to do just this. One of my favourite collections is of small light globes, balls of string and old locks and keys. Serviette rings are something I rarely use, but inside a large glass vase they look so impressive, and it brings

them out of hiding. If colour is your thing, reels of coloured cotton and wool look fun, as does a collection of old matchboxes from your favourite bars or restaurants. Once you start playing with ideas like this, you will be inspired every time you're at the haberdashery or hardware store.

THE PANTRY

 There is something about opening the pantry when it's just been cleaned and organised that fills you with a sense of calm. Having a well organised, totally functional pantry is a must-have in this busy day and age. All it takes is an hour of your time, some matching containers and a little pantry inspiration.

I am a firm believer that if you can see everything, you won't waste it. Shallow shelving will stop you from stockpiling cans; simple, clear containers will tell you when you are running low on items, and baskets are handy for odd-shaped packets that are a little tricky to decanter. I like to keep everything together – my herbs, spices and baking items, such as flour and sugars, all lined up neatly, a section for tea, and so on. Doing this makes it much easier to find what I am looking for in a hurry.

Learn to love labels

I can't be the only one who's confused plain (all-purpose) flour with self-raising flour, or icing (confectioners') sugar with cornflour. Poor labelling can cause some real issues in the kitchen, so there's no excuse not to label your jars, especially when there are so many free templates on the internet to get you started.

TIPS FOR A NEAT PANTRY

❖ When buying containers for your pantry, stick to the same size, style and look. Consistency with your containers will create an inviting sense of order.

❖ Label, label, label!

❖ Group similar items, especially oils and condiments, together so that you can see everything at once.

❖ Never store more than two layers deep. If you can't see it, you won't use it.

❖ Invest in good lighting for a walk-in pantry. Searching in the dark is no fun.

❖ Tidy weekly to avoid your pantry getting disorganised.

❖ Having a collection of baskets on the floor of a walk-in pantry is a neat and tidy way to store big packets and odd-shaped containers.

❖ A plastic-sleeved folder will solve your recipe mess. Simply slip cut-outs into a plastic sleeve and file away. Do the same with takeaway menus.

CREATIVE LABELLING

• Hang a simple piece of brown card from the lid and neatly write the contents in thick black marker.

• Paint a square on the outside of your jars with blackboard paint and label them with chalk.

• Write directly on the jar with a marker in neat, cursive writing.

• Match your labels to your kitchen colour scheme to ensure continuity.

THE LAUNDRY

> " Your laundry should be as minimal, clean and organised as possible. Yes, I know it's a drag of a room and no one wants to be in there for long, but there are ways to make the laundry a more hospitable space. Fill large glass jars with bulk items like buttons, threads, pegs and twine and put them on display for a stylish touch. It's so easy to recreate this look and add a little style to an otherwise drab space.

LAUNDRY TIPS

❖ Keep your laundry as minimal as possible, with no fuss and no mess.

❖ Use a collection of baskets to separate colours, dry-cleanable items, ironing etc.

❖ Keep a basket for items that need to be darned and next time you are sitting in front of the TV, mend those holes.

❖ Store spare buttons in a jar so they are always close at hand.

❖ Keep a piggy bank for loose change that falls out of pockets.

❖ Use a small laundry bag to store all those stray socks whose partners will eventually turn up.

❖ Have washing labels on display so you can see how to care for each item at a glance.

❖ Always fold your jumpers away – never hang them on coat hangers.

❖ Keep whites white by soaking your clothes for 10 minutes in a bucket of hot water with two sliced lemons.

❖ Always clean stains immediately (see page 53 for stain removal tips).

❖ Try and clean your clothes with natural cleaners, like vinegar, bicarbonate of soda (baking soda) and lemon.

❖ Always handwash your delicates.

❖ If buying detergent, make sure you buy the right one for the right fabric to ensure your clothes' longevity.

❖ When handwashing your knits, never wring them out as they will lose their shape. Instead, roll them up in a towel to squeeze the excess water out.

WASHING YOUR WOOLLIES

 As autumn ends, we start preparing for the winter months and that means freshening up our winter woollies. Make sure you read all washing instructions before washing any wool garments. For items that need a little softening, why not make your own detergent?

4 cups Lux soap flakes

250 ml (8½ fl oz/1 cup) methylated spirits

200 ml (7 fl oz) eucalyptus oil

—

MAKES 500 ML (17 FL OZ/2 CUPS)

Mix all the ingredients together in a large jar and leave until it sets to a jelly-like consistency. Use 1 tablespoon per load.

DRESSING ROOM

 My dressing room is my favourite space in our home. I love that I can see everything I own, and I have worked hard to make it the beautiful space it is. Even if you don't have a designated dressing room or walk-in wardrobe, storing your clothing and accessories correctly is very important.

What I love about open cupboards is that I am able to see everything easily, at a glance. But of course, this means I have to be tidy. To keep order, I colour-block all my clothing and try to keep certain things together like pants, jackets and long dresses. I also colour-block scarves and bags so I can see all my options and wear everything I have.

Matching coat hangers are a must in open cupboards. I use thin black velvet ones that allow me to hang more clothes and will hold my silk shirts and pants without them slipping off. I also go through all my clothes twice yearly and give away what I no longer wear. It's important to be ruthless in deciding what you actually wear in your wardrobe. Give away to friends or donate to charity anything that is taking up wasted space in your wardrobe. Ask yourself: 'What am I no longer wearing? What needs mending? What needs dry cleaning?' I find that asking myself these questions keeps me on my toes and helps me to not buy things I don't need. Haha ... That's a joke! There are pieces in my wardrobe that have been with me for years, so hold on to what is dear to you, whether it's on-trend or not.

 Jewellery is an obsession of mine and being able to see it all clearly ensures I never forget what I have. Lining your drawers (or jewellery box) with rubber matting will keep your jewellery from tangling and sliding around. I also colour-block and group similar collections for ease and efficiency. Larger accessories, like my collection of belts, sneakers and sandals, are kept together in large, clear Perspex boxes, this way you can see inside and easily find what you are looking for.

Sunglasses are something I like to keep out on display too, so I can see what I have. I love the look of displaying them on beautiful trays. Leaving certain accessories out on display adds a little character and a personal touch.

It's not all about storage though, you want the space to look good as well. I decided to have large shelves installed over my couch so that I could colour block all my pale pink things together. I created different collections and incorporated old books, antique tiaras and a portrait of my mother. It means I'm making use of all my available space, plus, it looks like an art installation!

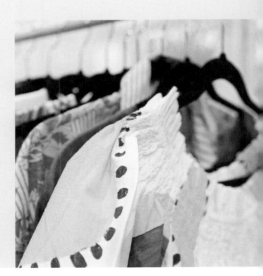

WIN

TER

WINTER IS THE TIME FOR HOME

" To enjoy winter, you need to layer up your home, just like you do with your clothes. As much as the cold makes me feel alive, there is something so lovely about turning into our driveway, seeing the house all lit up and knowing it will be warm and cosy inside. Winter is the perfect time to add blankets and throws to your beds and couches, light the candles to create a romantic glow, and fill the fridge with warm, hearty comfort food. Have a bright coat handy, and a comfortable pair of boots, and you will survive even the coldest of days.

ORCHIDS

" My love affair with flowers started early on. As a child, I was fascinated by the variety of orchids my grandmother had growing in her glasshouse. So much so that I was given a book of botanical drawings of orchids when I was eight. I would spend hours tracing the pages in the book, trying to draw the perfect flower.

Orchids are amazing plants that thrive in the heat of a warm house in winter. They are also the gift that keeps on giving as, once the flowers die off, you can move your orchid outside until next winter, when it will bloom again for all to enjoy.

ORCHIDS ON THE TABLE

For this winter setting, I wanted to create a warm and moody feel using wood, leather and dark metal trinkets, with the orchids bringing the look together and complementing the beautiful Suzani throw hanging on my wall. While buying orchids from florists can be expensive, you do get longer life out of them as they thrive in the indoor warmth.

SECRET TIP

Don't be scared to use faux orchids in the foliage once the original orchid has died. I do this all the time, and no one can ever tell the difference.

To get this look, I divided one long orchid stem into three shorter sections of 2–3 flowers each, and also cut individual flowers off the stalk to use as place settings, and to float in water.
I wanted to add something personal and create a unique twist, so I layered up personal items among the vases. This is a good way to create talking points for guests – they will ask where different things are from. You should always have talking points on your table; something unusual to spark a conversation, but don't let them distract from the focus of the table, which is, of course, orchids.

This lush winter table setting is completed by gold cutlery, chocolate-brown linen napkins, simple gold-rimmed white plates and an eclectic selection of glassware, with a few dark-brown candles to create a moody glow. When you're done setting a table, always stand back to look at the overall balance. What else can you use to add some interest? Half the fun of putting together a table like this is finding treasures around your house to display and share with your guests.

WINTER WONDERS

Orchids just say winter to me. The cymbidium variety in particular comes in beautiful, warm earthy tones, with lush green foliage – perfect for adding winter colour to your home. Potted orchids have a different look and feel to cut flowers and will thrive in a heated winter home considerably longer than flowers in a vase. They can also be planted in a variety of beautiful decorative containers, adding another dimension to your home's winter decor. They do need natural light and air though, so make sure you sit them in a bright space. If this isn't possible, give them a few hours in the sun once a week. They will thank you for it with large, dramatic blooms in moody wintry tones.

I always repot my orchids into beautiful glass vases when I bring them home. Doing this is a little bit fiddly but it looks great. If replanting into a larger vase than the pot it came in, you will need extra potting mix to bring the soil level up. Make sure you use a potting mix specifically designed for orchids, and don't overwater the plant. Glass vases don't have drainage holes like other plant containers, so a little spray or dribble of water every few days will do the trick. To finish off my potted orchids, I like to place fresh moss on top of the soil. You can even keep the orchid in the plastic container it came in. Just cover the outside of it with moss and place it inside your glass vase.

HOW TO REPOT AN ORCHID

◈ Choose a pot or vase that is a little larger than the original, but not too big. Orchids like to have their roots snug.

◈ Pull the pot away from the plant and wash the roots under running water.

◈ With very sharp scissors or secateurs, cut off any brown or rotting roots.

◈ Fill the base of your new pot or vase with orchid potting mix (available from all nurseries). Put your orchid in place and fill your pot with extra orchid potting mix.

◈ Place in a well-lit position.

POTTED ORCHID TIPS

◈ As much as you will be tempted to, don't water them too much. Once or twice a week is fine.

◈ If you do overwater, let the soil dry out completely then give your orchid a small drink once a week.

◈ Keep your orchid away from excessive heat and chill. They last longer in a mild, warm environment.

◈ After your orchid blooms, snip off the old flower spike, near the base of the plant. This will encourage growth for the next season and keep your plant looking clean.

◈ If your orchid's leaves turn yellow or it isn't blooming, move it to a lighter space. It may not have found its favourite spot yet. When it does it will reward you with blooms.

WHISKEY BAR

Winter reminds me of my grandparents and of all the time I spent with them when I was growing up. My grandfather had the most fantastic bar, with ice at the ready and nuts in a bowl. When he came home at the end of the day, he always poured himself a whiskey in the same cut-crystal glass. It was like poetry in motion.

Not many of us have space for a built-in bar, but a drinks cart is something most people can fit in their home. I love the idea of a whiskey cart stocked with a variety of different decanters and whiskey bottles, all layered up with beautiful cut-crystal glasses.

Having mixers and a bowl of ice on hand makes it easy to pour yourself, or your guests, the perfect drink. Style the cart with an orchid planted in a glass vase with some moss on the surface. It's always fun to add a bit of drama to cocktail hour!

ESPRESSO OLD FASHIONED

A drinks cart calls for a delicious, whiskey-based cocktail, and what could be more perfect at the end of a cold winter's day than an Old Fashioned, with an espresso twist and an orchid for garnish, of course.

60 ml (2 fl oz/¼ cup) double-shot espresso, cooled to room temperature

30 ml (1 fl oz) rye whiskey

15 ml (½ fl oz) sugar syrup (page 99)

dash of Angostura bitters

lemon peel

—

SERVES 1

Combine the espresso, rye whiskey, sugar syrup and bitters in a cocktail shaker and fill with ice.

Shake until the outside of the shaker is frosty, about 30 seconds. Strain into a rocks glass filled with ice.

Twist the lemon peel over the cocktail to release its oils, then rub it over the rim of the glass. Discard the peel.

For an extra-special look, garnish with an orchid head like I have! (Most common orchids are non-toxic, but do check your variety's toxicity first.)

OLIVES

" Hills covered in olive trees are one of my favourite sights when travelling through Europe. I love the trees' shape and colour, and a picnic underneath olive tree branches heavy with bright green fruit is a great way to unwind and relax. Olives come in a large number of tasty varieties, and ending the day with a glass of wine and some delicious marinated olives is just perfection.

A PICNIC
IN THE
OLIVE
GROVE

Sometimes, we get a little lazy and don't make enough time for special moments. I say we should, because that's how we make beautiful memories – and don't do things halfway, go all out. Whether you're creating a romantic atmosphere for two or enjoying an afternoon in the sun with all your friends, make an effort. Sure, we don't all have easy access to an olive grove; the point here is to find a location you love and create something special. Whether it's the local park or your own garden, nature's colours are always a great source of inspiration.

It's best to work with the colours around you when styling outdoors. My afternoon picnic in the olive grove was inspired by the blue hues of olives and the tonal greens of olive branches, so I used teal blankets and cushions that mirror the colours of the grove. You could set this up any time of year, but in the midst of winter, olive trees are full of fruit and the branches look amazing.

And what does one eat when sitting in a rustic olive grove? Well, there are many things the humble olive can produce.

OLIVE TAPENADE

125 g (4½ oz/1 cup) good-quality kalamata olives, pitted

4 anchovies, drained

1 small garlic clove, chopped

1 tablespoon capers, drained

60 ml (2 fl oz/¼ cup) extra-virgin olive oil

juice of ½ lemon

freshly ground black pepper

—

MAKES 250 G (9 OZ)

Place the olives, anchovies, garlic and capers in a small food processor. Process until the mixture is almost smooth. With the motor running, slowly add the oil in a thin, steady stream until the mixture forms a thick, smooth paste. (Adding the oil slowly prevents the tapenade from separating.)

Transfer the tapenade to a small bowl and stir in 2 teaspoons of the lemon juice, or more if desired. Season with pepper, serve and enjoy.

To store excess tapenade, transfer it to a sterilised glass jar or container. Pour over enough extra-virgin olive oil to cover the surface and refrigerate for up to 1 week.

YUMMY OLIVE BREAD

Best purchased fresh from your favourite bakery, warm olive bread is delicious when served with good olive oil and rock salt, although olive bread with vegemite and lashings of butter is my absolute favourite. It's a big hit of salty goodness, but I love it. Avocado mash is also nice as it softens the saltiness of the olives with its creamy texture. For a double-dose of delicious olive flavour, try it with beautiful tapenade.

LEMON & ROSEMARY OLIVE OIL CAKE

This dense olive oil cake is the perfect afternoon treat for anyone with a sweet tooth. It's simple, fresh and deliciously moist. Olive oil can be used for most baked recipes and is a healthier alternative to butter.

380 g (13½ oz/2½ cups) plain (all-purpose) flour, plus 2 tablespoons for dusting

1½ tablespoons finely chopped fresh rosemary

2 teaspoons baking powder

½ teaspoon bicarbonate of soda (baking soda)

½ teaspoon salt

345 g (12 oz/1½ cups) caster (superfine) sugar

125 ml (4 fl oz/½ cup) olive oil

125 ml (4 fl oz/½ cup) skim milk

zest of 1 lemon

60 ml (2 fl oz/¼ cup) fresh lemon juice, plus 1 tablespoon for the icing

½ teaspoon vanilla extract

¼ teaspoon lemon extract

3 large eggs

125 g (4½ oz/1 cup) icing (confectioners') sugar, sieved

olive branches or rosemary sprigs, to garnish (optional)

—

SERVES 8–16

Preheat the oven to 180°C (350°F).

Grease a 25 cm (10 in) round cake tin with olive oil spray and dust it with 2 tablespoons of flour.

In a large mixing bowl, combine the flour, rosemary, baking powder, bicarbonate of soda and salt.

In another bowl, combine the caster sugar, olive oil, milk, lemon zest, lemon juice, vanilla and lemon extracts and eggs. Whisk at a low speed for two minutes, or until smooth.

Add the wet ingredients to the flour mixture and beat with a mixer at low speed until blended.

Pour the batter into your prepared tin and bake for 45 minutes, or until a skewer inserted in the centre comes out clean.

Remove from the pan and cool for 15 minutes on a wire rack.

To make the icing, combine the icing sugar and the tablespoon of lemon juice. Stir until smooth and pour evenly over the cake.

Garnish with an olive branch or a rosemary sprig.

INFUSED OLIVE OIL

 Olives are a versatile fruit usually grown from grafted plants. When taken care of, an olive tree can last for centuries.

Olive oil is created by pressing the fruit. It can then be flavoured by infusing it with herbs and spices. You can easily infuse olive oil yourself, to use in salads, marinades and, of course, cooking. And how lovely it is to have homemade oil on the table when friends come over for lunch, or to give it away as a present. You can buy beautiful bottles to use for your infusions.

Fun olive oil infusions

Chilli: 1 tablespoon dried chili flakes or 4 medium-sized, sliced fresh chillies.

Lemon and pepper: 4 slices of lemon and 12 peppercorns.

Rosemary and garlic: 2 long rosemary sprigs and 2 small bulbs of garlic, halved.

Basil and garlic: 4 sprigs of basil and 2 small bulbs of garlic, halved.

–

FOR 500 ML (17 FL OZ/2 CUPS) EXTRA-VIRGIN OLIVE OIL

Make sure your bottle is sterilised (see page 37), dry and has a good seal. If you are infusing herbs, bruise them gently to release some of their oil. For spices, you can lightly toast them first. For lemon or fresh chilli, slice them thinly.

Place the flavours inside your empty bottle, then fill it with good-quality extra-virgin olive oil. Seal and leave the bottle in the pantry for a few weeks before using, to give the flavour enough time to infuse.

MUSHROOMS

" I've always been fascinated by mushrooms – by how they look, and by their odd colours and shapes. And then, of course, there is the well-known fact that fairies live underneath mushrooms, which gives them a magical quality and puts a smile on my face whenever I see a mushroom circle growing in the wild.

A WHIMSICAL MUSHROOM TABLE SETTING

 Inspiration for this picture-perfect winter setting came from the gorgeousness that is a field of mushrooms. The table features oversized velvet mushrooms I found in a novelty gift shop, surrounded by greenery to create a little indoor field of mushrooms.

STYLING TIP

When styling any table, collect everything you need before you get started. There is nothing more annoying than being halfway through setting up only to find your glassware doesn't quite match. Do a little stocktake: is all the crockery clean? Do you have enough? Are your napkins ironed? Do you have enough cutlery for the number of courses you are serving? Is everything polished?

The colour of the velvet inspired this entire table; everything from the colour of the napkins to the plates and chairs. To add some interest and detail, I dotted around a few punnets of perennials from my local nursery and stuck some smaller faux mushrooms from a craft store in them to complete my garden scene.

I wanted a consistent colour palette for this setting, so I needed a table and chairs that matched. A simple furniture swap can really bring a space to life and if you don't have what you need in your home, you can always hire. I used a collection of eclectic cutlery for my place settings. Don't feel you have to use matching cutlery sets; a mix-and-match approach works well for a table setting like this and adds a rustic touch. Pale orange glassware, tied in with the napkins, keeps it all clean and simple, with the focus on those amazing velveteen mushrooms. It's a calm winter look that calls for a delicious and healthy menu.

COMMON MUSHROOM TYPES

Button: These mushrooms have a firm, delicate texture and a mild flavour that intensifies when cooked. They can be eaten raw but are one of the most versatile mushrooms to cook with.

Field: The caps of these mushrooms open out flat and have a dark underside with a spongy texture. They have an intense, almost 'meaty' flavour and are good for roasting or barbecuing.

Portobello: These dense, firm, meaty-textured mushrooms have a rich flavour and are ideal for grilling, roasting or on the barbecue as a vegetarian option.

Swiss brown: Dark brown in colour, these mushrooms hold their shape well when cooked and have an earthy flavour ideal for pasta, risottos, pies and curries.

Chestnut: With their long, creamy coloured stalks, chestnut mushrooms have a strong, nutty flavour. They are the perfect breakfast mushroom and are delicious sautéed with butter, garlic and thyme.

Enoki: This is a Japanese variety with long, thread-like edible stems topped with a tiny button cap. They can be eaten raw or cooked. Separate before serving in salads, sandwiches or rice paper rolls, or add to soups, omelettes or risottos just before serving.

Shiitake: These mushrooms have a meaty texture and flavour, and a distinctive smell. A shiitake's flavour intensifies the longer it's cooked. Match them with strong-flavoured meats like duck, venison or aged beef. Also suitable for stir-fries, braises, soups and sauces.

HOW TO CARE FOR MUSHROOMS

❖ Store fresh mushrooms, unwashed, in a paper bag for up to 3 days. Storing them in plastic will cause them to sweat.

❖ To clean mushrooms, wipe them down gently with a damp paper towel one at a time. Do not soak them in water as they are very absorbent and won't cook properly if waterlogged.

❖ Always cut your mushrooms with a sharp knife. Serrated knifes will bruise them.

PICKLED MUSHROOMS

Marinated and preserved mushrooms are delicious. There are so many different types out there, so step out of your comfort zone and have a play by mixing in various herbs to find your favourite combination. Pickled mushrooms are great for adding to sauces, pasta dishes, risottos and that perfectly cooked steak. A jar of pickled mushrooms in your pantry is a great staple to have on hand for those nights when you need a quick and tasty meal.

750 g (1 lb 11 oz) mushrooms

3 thyme sprigs, or herbs of choice

1 small spring onion (scallion), thinly sliced

1½ teaspoons whole allspice

1 tablespoon whole black peppercorns

3 bay leaves

1 tablespoon sea salt

80 ml (2½ fl oz/⅓ cup) white-wine vinegar

185 ml (6 fl oz/¾ cup) water

—

**MAKES 1 MEDIUM-SIZED JAR
(APPROX 450 G/1 LB)**

Wash the mushrooms by quickly running them under cold water, then pat them dry with paper towel. Slice smaller mushrooms in half and larger ones in quarters.

Place the thyme sprigs into a sterilised mason jar (see page 37 on how to sterilise jars).

Combine the mushrooms and all remaining ingredients in a medium saucepan and bring to the boil. Reduce the heat and simmer for 15 minutes.

Pour the hot mushrooms and liquid into the jar and leave to cool. When the mushrooms are cool, seal the jar and place it in the fridge. The mushrooms will be ready to eat after 3 days and will last in the fridge for up to 1 month.

MUSHROOM PIZZA

This recipe is a delicious way to use up a glut of mushrooms. Add as much or as little of the topping ingredients as you want, to suit your taste.

Pizza dough

1¼ teaspoons active dried yeast

½ teaspoon sugar

1 teaspoon sea salt

1 tablespoon extra-virgin olive oil

335 g (12 oz/2¼ cups) cups unbleached bread flour

extra flour for dusting and for shaping the dough

Mushroom topping

2 tablespoons unsalted butter

3 tablespoons extra-virgin olive oil

450 g (1 lb) shiitake mushrooms, stems removed and caps cut into quarters

450 g (1 lb) oyster mushrooms, stalks removed and torn into 2.5 cm (1 in) pieces

225 g (8 oz) whole brown beech mushrooms, stalks trimmed

½ teaspoon sea salt

freshly ground black pepper

Additional toppings

250 g (9 oz) garlic confit (see page 198)

375 g (13 oz/1½ cups) ricotta (buffalo mozzarella is a good substitute)

3 tablespoons rosemary, coarsely chopped

sea salt and freshly ground black pepper to taste

65 g (2¼ oz/⅔ cup) parmesan shavings, to garnish

garlic-infused oil (from the confit), for garnish

To make the dough, combine the yeast and sugar in a medium bowl. Pour 250 ml (8½ fl oz/1 cup) warm water over the yeast and sugar and whisk until the yeast dissolves. Let stand for 5–10 minutes. When the yeast activates (it will start to bubble up to the surface), whisk in the salt and olive oil. Add the flour and stir with a wooden spoon until the dough comes together.

Turn the dough out onto your work surface and start kneading it. If it sticks, add a little flour and try to knead a little faster. Kneading too slowly causes the dough to stick, but you still want it to be slightly sticky to yield a delicious, light pizza crust, so it's crucial to get the balance right at this step. Don't add too much flour or the dough will be firmer and harder to shape and the crust will be stiff. Continue kneading the dough for 8–10 minutes until smooth and elastic.

Roll the dough in flour until well dusted and place in a large bowl. Cover the bowl with plastic wrap and leave in a warm place for 1 hour, or until doubled in size.

Divide the dough in half and shape each half into a ball. Roll the balls in flour again, place each ball in a medium bowl and cover with plastic wrap. Refrigerate for a minimum of 3 hours (max. 36 hours) before making your pizzas.

When you're ready to make your pizzas, roll out the dough into a round pizza base approximately 30 cm (12 in) in diameter and 1–2 cm (½–¾ in) thick.

To make the mushroom topping, melt the butter in a large non-stick frying pan over a high heat. Once the butter has melted, add the oil and shiitake mushrooms and toss, spreading evenly over the whole surface of the pan. Sauté for 2 minutes or until the mushrooms have wilted and begun to turn golden. Add the oyster and beech mushrooms to the pan and toss well. Continue to sauté on a high heat until the mushrooms are golden brown. Add the salt and pepper to taste and transfer to a bowl.

Preheat the oven to 260°C (500°F). Place your prepared pizza dough on a greased baking tray ready to load with toppings. (Make sure you only use half the ingredients in the list for the first pizza to make sure you leave enough ingredients for the second.)

Blend the garlic confit to a paste and spread it over the pizza base, almost to the edge.

Top with the mushroom topping, and sprinkle with ricotta, rosemary and a pinch of salt and pepper.

Slide the pizza tray into the hot oven and bake for 3–4 minutes, until the crust is browned on the edges.

Once cooked, remove from the oven and garnish with the parmesan shavings. Drizzle with the garlic-infused oil to taste and serve immediately.

GARLIC CONFIT

Whether you add it to a grilled-cheese sandwich, mashed potatoes or tomato soup, garlic confit is the perfect way to take your culinary creations to the next level and to use up a glut of olive oil. This garlic and olive oil infusion can be used as a condiment, as the base of a sauce or simply spread lavishly on a piece of hot crusty bread.

cloves of 5 large garlic bulbs, peeled, with root end trimmed off

360 ml (12 fl oz) extra-virgin olive oil

–

MAKES 250 G (9 OZ)

Place the garlic cloves and oil in a heavy-bottomed saucepan. The oil should cover the cloves by about 1 cm (½ in).

Heat over a low heat until the oil reaches between 93–99°C (199–210°F) when tested with a cooking thermometer. Small bubbles will come to the surface, but make sure the oil never comes to a boil.

Reduce the heat to maintain the temperature between 93–99°C (199–210°F) and slowly simmer the garlic for around 1 hour, until the cloves are completely tender and pale-golden in colour.

Remove the pan from the heat and allow the confit to cool to room temperature.

Transfer the garlic and oil to an airtight container and refrigerate for up to 1 month. Be sure to bring the confit to room temperature before using, as the oil will firm up when refrigerated.

MUSHROOM & PANCETTA SPAGHETTI

400 g (14 oz) spaghetti

60 ml (2 fl oz/¼ cup) olive oil

400 g (14 oz) cup mushrooms, sliced

8 slices pancetta, chopped

3 eggs

3 tablespoons flat-leaf (Italian) parsley, chopped

50 g (1¾ oz/½ cup) parmesan cheese, finely grated

sea salt

freshly ground black pepper

–

SERVES 4

Cook the spaghetti according to the packet instructions in a large saucepan of salted water.

Meanwhile, heat the oil in a large frying pan over a medium–high heat. Add the mushrooms and pancetta and cook, stirring occasionally, for 5 minutes, or until the pancetta is crisp.

Drain the spaghetti and return it to the saucepan.

Whisk the eggs in a bowl until well combined.

Add the eggs, mushroom mixture and parsley to the spaghetti and toss until well combined.

Return the saucepan to the heat for about 1 minute and toss until the egg begins to set.

Remove from the heat, and season with the parmesan and salt and pepper.

Serve immediately.

MUSHROOM FETA TART

2 sheets (approx. 100 g/3½ oz) frozen puff pastry, partially thawed

1 egg, lightly beaten

1 tablespoon olive oil

1½ tablespoons butter

4 eschalots, finely sliced

1 garlic clove, thinly sliced

200 g (7 oz/2¼ cups) button mushrooms, quartered

200 g (7 oz/2¼ cups) cup mushrooms, sliced

1 tablespoon fresh thyme leaves, chopped

50 g (1¾ oz/⅓ cup) feta, crumbled

fresh thyme leaves and salad leaves, to serve

–

SERVES 4–6

Preheat a fan-forced oven to 200°C (400°F) and line a 28 cm (11 in) pie tin with baking paper. Layer both pastry sheets over the tin and push the pastry into the edges. Using a sharp knife, trim off any excess pastry. Prick the centre with a fork and brush it with the egg. Cover with baking paper and baking weights (e.g. baking beads or uncooked rice). Blind-bake for 10 minutes, or until light golden and puffed.

Meanwhile, heat the oil and butter in a saucepan over a medium–high heat. Add the eschalots and garlic and cook, stirring, for 2 minutes, or until fragrant. Add the mushrooms and thyme, and season with salt and pepper. Cook, stirring, for 6–8 minutes, or until the mushrooms are tender and the liquid has almost evaporated. Remove from the heat.

Transfer the mushroom mixture to the pastry and top with the crumbled feta. Bake for 15 minutes, or until golden and puffed. Stand for 2 minutes before sprinkling with thyme and serving.

MERINGUE MUSHROOMS

This is such a cute, whimsical dessert that you can plate up any way you like. They look delightful with some raspberries and fresh cream, garnished with mint.

2 egg whites

¼ teaspoon cream of tartar

¼ teaspoon salt

1 teaspoon vanilla extract

230 g (8 oz /1 cup) caster (superfine) sugar

1 tablespoon Dutch (unsweetened) cocoa powder

110 g (4 oz) dark (semi-sweet) cooking chocolate (block or drops)

—

MAKES 8–12

Preheat the oven to 110°C (230°F) and line two baking trays with baking paper.

In a large mixing bowl, whisk the egg whites until foamy. Add the cream of tartar, salt and vanilla and continue whisking to form soft peaks. Gradually sprinkle in the sugar so it doesn't sink to the bottom. Continue whisking until the mixture holds stiff, shiny peaks.

Place the meringue mixture into a piping (icing) bag with a round tip. For the mushroom caps, pipe round blobs of meringue onto one of the prepared baking trays. To ensure a smooth round top, pull the bag off to the side while piping to avoid making peaks.

Pipe the stems onto the second tray. Squeeze out a small blob of meringue, then pull the piping bag straight up. They should resemble candy kisses. Don't stress about making the pieces exactly the same, you want to make them look organic and natural, like real mushrooms.

Dust the mushroom caps with cocoa powder using a small sifter, then bake for 1 hour, or until the caps are dry enough to be removed easily from the baking tray. Set aside to cool.

Melt the chocolate in a metal bowl over simmering water, or in a glass bowl in the microwave, stirring occasionally until smooth.

Poke a small hole in the bottom of a mushroom cap. Spread chocolate over the bottom of the cap. Dip the tip of a meringue stem in chocolate, and press lightly into the hole. When the chocolate sets, they will hold together. Repeat with the remaining pieces.

Store your meringue mushrooms at room temperature in a dry place, or in a tin.

BOOKS & FIREPLACES

66 In winter, my idea of heaven is to lie on a couch in front of a beautiful, fragrant fire, read a new favourite book and watch the flames dance in the fireplace. I love to incorporate books into my styling around the house – they give personality to a home, tell us a lot about their owners and make a great talking point.

STYLING
YOUR HOME
WITH BOOKS

 A house says a lot about its owner and a house filled with books is a home full of character and warmth. Books are something I just can't have enough of; it's an addiction. Not only do I always have a few novels on the go, but I am also a huge collector of coffee table books about flowers, gardening and decorating. Styling your bookshelves to fit with your decor is an effortless way to make a statement. Whether it's colour-blocking or putting books together by size, you can have so much fun planning and creating.

The number of times I have been sitting and watching TV, only to glance across at my bookcase and find myself still moving books around two hours later! No one else notices except me, but I like my bookshelves to be just right and pleasing to the eye. Books are also an excellent way to provide height on a sideboard or table, or place under a vase or lamp. A stack of books is also a straightforward way to elevate decorative items. Choose book spines that work with what you are lifting and keep the sizes relatively the same.

Don't just leave your books on the shelf, get creative and turn your collection into an installation. Books are a versatile decorating tool and styling them is a fun way to enjoy a lazy Sunday.

BOOK STYLING TIPS

❖ If you have a neutral space and don't necessarily want your books on display, style with the colour of the 'naked' pages. Fantastic en masse, this look is simple and effective. All you need to do is carefully rip the covers off and remove as much glue residue as you can to keep them neat. Then simply pile the books high with the spines facing you, so all you can see is a neutral colour palette – as easy as that.

❖ Display your books like art by colour coding them and keeping each block a different tone. Colour coding books on white shelving creates a stunning effect and can make a room feel so much more eclectic. Organise your books by spine colour and size, then arrange them back on your shelves. Working through the colours of the rainbow, gradually moving from one colour to the next, creates a beautiful effect.

❖ Don't forget to show off some of your gorgeous covers. We are so used to just displaying the spines that the covers often get forgotten, only to be seen when the book is picked up and read. Turn a selection of your books to the front to display their covers in all their glory.

❖ Fill the corners of your house with a curated selection of books. I like to colour-block piles around the house – some tables have a selection of red spines, while lifestyle books are sometimes just piles of white. You get the idea. This is ideal for coffee tables, side tables and tricky corners that need a stylish lift.

CREATE
A MASCULINE
OFFICE
SPACE

 My home is my haven and I love nothing more than decorating and rearranging. There is a lot of my style and layering around the home, so I felt it was important to create a space just for the men in my family, to give them a place that they would love to be in, and work in. In this day and age, we often have just a computer on our desks, so it's good to layer up and create extra warmth in the office space.

A leather tray for bills and mail will keep everything in order, while printing off some of your favourite photographs and putting them in matching frames is a special way to personalise a workspace. There are a few other things that are useful on our desks: a container for a collection of pencils plus a beautiful leather notebook, along with a letter opener, looks great. Help your family stay organised by having everything within arm's reach, including envelopes, business cards and stamps.

Using bookshelves layered with eclectic ornaments and books will immediately make a room feel more intimate. Books say so much about the person who owns them and their style, so they need to be on display. If I had my way, I would have books in every room.

For a masculine space, leather-bound books are my go-to. I love the dark, rich leather covers that almost appear like a wall of leather when shelved in a series. Leather creates a dark,

moody feel that is perfect for winter. Leather, wood and dark metals look great together, and work well layered with different fabrics and textures. A shelf with old leather books and collected knick-knacks is a good way of creating a masculine display in your office, study or nook.

SAVE ME
A SPOT BY
THE FIRE

 Having a fireplace is such a luxury, particularly in winter. But for many years, we never lit our fireplace at home purely because we thought it was too hard to organise firewood and keep it clean. How silly is that? Even though we didn't have a fire in it, I decided I couldn't let it sit there, bare and unused. I styled it with other things to create a delightful ornamental nook in the house. If you decide you don't want to use your fireplace, try popping the following inside instead:

◆ Perfectly cut silver birch logs. You don't have to light them, they're just pretty to look at.

◆ A variety of candles of different heights. Light them all to create a gorgeous glow without the mess.

◆ A collection of old books. Wrap some piles of books with twine and fill up the fireplace.

◆ Antlers anyone? It's incredible what you can find and be creative with. Have fun with it.

CARING FOR YOUR FIREPLACE

❖ Clear your mantle and surrounds of any decorations that pose a fire hazard (vases, photo frames and the like are fine) and move furniture a little further away to give the fire some space.

❖ Only burn old, dried wood – six months to a year old, at least.

❖ Make sure there are no branches outside near your chimney.

❖ Make sure your chimney is covered with wire mesh to keep out birds and other animals.

❖ To avoid excess smoke in the house, burn your wood on a raised grate towards the back of your fireplace.

❖ Always put out your fire before going to bed, just in case.

❖ A mesh or glass fire guard will stop embers from escaping.

FIREWOOD

" Who knew not all firewood is the same?
Not me. I knew the basics, like don't use
green wood and start your fire with kindling,
not liquid accelerants. But I didn't know
that different wood gives out different
levels of heat.

It's simple: softwoods (cypress, cedar, red pine,
fir) are light and catch fire easily. They also
burn faster and cleaner. Hardwoods (blackbutt,
grey box, ironbark, oak, maple, beech, elm)
are heavier, burn twice as long and generate
twice the heat. Stocking your woodpile with a
good amount of kindling and a combination
of hardwood and softwood will help you get a
roaring fire going in no time.

FRAGRANT FIRES

You can get some great scents coming from your hearth once the fireplace is packed with wood and ready to go. Whether you like it sweet or earthy, this is a lovely alternative to scented candles.

◈ **Rosemary:** This aromatic herb can be dried out and burnt as kindling, emitting a glorious smell. You can even place bundles around the fire. It smells gorgeous once warmed up.

◈ **Orange and lemon peel:** Burning citrus peel is an excellent way to get rid of odours in the home. The oils in the peel give out a lovely, clean smell.

◈ **Cinnamon:** It creates a sweet smell, and because cinnamon spice is actually the inner bark of a tree, it burns very well.

◈ **Pine cones:** A favourite to burn for its fresh pine smell. Just make sure you use dried old cones – they burn best.

◈ **Essential oils:** Choose your favourite aroma and put a few drops on the wood. Let it dry before burning. A subtle, fragrant fire, how fab!

CANDLES

Candles are a wonderful way to create a warm, wintry glow in the home. Turn off your overhead lights and instead light lots of candles to create a moody, cosy space. If you don't have enough candleholders, use old vases. Tea light candles are an inexpensive way to create a romantic, candle-lit atmosphere and can be placed in a collection of drinking glasses.

Fragrant candles are something I absolutely love. I change mine for each room and each season. To me, winter is all about warm ambers and smokiness, while spring is about fragrant, floral scents.

QUICK TIPS FOR LOOKING AFTER CANDLES

◆ The first burn is critical. You need to burn your new candle for 2–3 hours to avoid a 'memory ring'. This is the small puddle that forms around the base of the wick. If you only burn it for a short amount of time, resulting in a small memory ring, the candle will burn like this for its entire life.

◆ After you blow out a candle and the wick has returned to room temperature, trim it to 5 mm (¼ in) at a 45-degree angle.

◆ Burn your candles carefully: keep them away from draughts, never leave them unattended and always sit them on a heat-resistant surface.

◆ Store unused candles in a cool, dry place away from direct sunlight to avoid them discolouring, fading or melting.

◆ If soot forms on the side of your candle, extinguish the flame, wipe it with a damp cloth, trim your wick and relight.

◆ Extinguish your candle if the flame flickers, burns too high or smokes. Let the candle cool, trim your wick and relight.

◆ To maximise the strength of your candle's scent, keep all doors and windows closed for at least 30 minutes.

GET COSY THIS WINTER

❖ Come winter, change your light bulbs to a lower wattage to create a cosier, more ambient atmosphere in your home. Light plays such a prominent role in our mood and coming home on a cold evening to a warm, glowing home can only ever be a good thing.

❖ Bring out extra cushions, throws and blankets. Drape them over the arms of your chairs and keep a few in some conveniently placed baskets in your sitting areas. You want a warm, cosy blanket to be in reach when you relax on the couch at night.

❖ Layer up and add more textures to your homewares in the way of rugs, weaved cushions, fur, tassels and wool to create the feeling of extra warmth.

❖ Create a nook in a sunny spot under the window to soak up that winter sun. All you need is a comfy chair, a side table full of magazines and a couple of throws and cushions.

❖ Surround yourself in softness. Fake fur throws and cushions, and sheepskin rugs will add that touch of luxury.

❖ If you have an open fire, arrange your furniture so it surrounds the hearth. Spend those cold nights snuggled up by the fire with loved ones.

INDEX

A

A green thumb's birthday 84–5
A picnic in the olive grove 180
A summer romance 68–9
A whimsical mushroom table setting 190–1
afternoon tea 68–75
anemones 28
arranging, flowers 27
artichoke dip, Autumn 137
Autumn artichoke dip 137
Autumnal crunch 140–1
avocadoes
  Avocado, tomato and cheese salad 102
  Quinoa, avocado and sweet corn salad 103

B

Barbecue, Peruvian 95
bed linen 55
  Homemade linen water 59
  How to fold a fitted sheet 58
  Tips and tricks 58
bedroom tips 55
bicarbonate of soda (baking soda) 50
Bloody Mary 90
books 205, 206, 209
  book styling tips 207
bouquets 18, 26, 28
bread, Yummy olive 183
Build a nest egg 46–7
bulbs 17, 18–9, 28
  growing 19
Buttercream 72
butter, Lemon 34

C

cakes
  Lemon and rosemary olive oil cake 184
  The semi-naked cake 72–5
candles 55, 120, 171, 210, 214–5
  quick tips for looking after candles 214
cheese salad, Avocado, tomato and 102
chicken
  Pollo a la brasa (Grilled chicken) 104

The perfect roast chicken 44–5
cleaning 38, 50–1
  ants 38
  brass 50
  butcher's block 38
  chrome 50
  cobwebs 52
  copper 50
  crystal 51
  fabric 50
  fridge 38
  garbage disposal 38
  glass 50
  glassware 52
  hacks 52
  kettle 52
  mirrors 50, 52
  natural 50
  outdoor cleaning 114
  plastic 38
  silver 50
  spring clean 49
  stainless steel 52
  stain removers 53
  tile grout 50
  white clothes 52
  wicker baskets 52
  wooden chopping board 38
cocktails
  Bloody Mary 90
  Espresso Old Fashioned 176
  Passionfruit Mojito 25
  Pisco Sour 99
  Rose Cocktail 77
colour 20, 24, 26, 42, 54, 68, 85, 96, 110, 120, 129, 141, 171, 180, 193
  colour-blocking 158, 207
confit, Garlic 198
Create a masculine office space 208–9
cushions 110–3, 215
cutlery 24, 42, 68, 149, 171, 193

D

daffodils 27
dahlias 28, 123
  Decorating with dahlias 128–9
  How to make a dahlia block 126–7
  Facts and tips 127
  Tea among the dahlias 124–5
Decorating with dahlias 128–9

delphiniums 28
dip, Autumn artichoke 137
Display your collections in clusters 150
dolmades, Greek 142
dogwood 28
dressing, Lime 137

E

eggs 41
  Build a nest egg 46–7
Espresso Old Fashioned 176
eucalyptus 28
euphorbia 28

F

feathers 41
  Build a nest egg 46–7
  Feather your nest 42–3
feta tart, Mushroom 201
ficus 28
fireplaces 205, 210, 215
  caring for your fireplace 211
  firewood 212
  fragrant fires 213
firewood 212
fitted sheet, How to fold a 58
floral foam 124
flower food 28
flowers
  arranging 27, 128
  cutting 28, 79
  preparation 28
  preserving 29
  pressing 81
  stems 28
food preparation 38
forget-me-nots 81
  How to press flowers 81
freesias 28
Freshen up your bedroom 54–5

G

garlic
  Garlic confit 198
  Infused olive oil 186
Get creative with autumn leaves 145
gifts 37, 46, 78, 85, 93, 144,
gin 37
  Rose cocktail 77
glassware 24, 51, 52, 111, 171, 175, 193, 214
  cleaning 52

Greek dolmades 142
Grilled lamb chops with herbs and
   spices 106
guest room, The 56–7

H
hellebores 27, 28
herbs 27, 85
   Grilled lamb chops with herbs and
      spices 106
   Peruvian green sauce 107
hollyhocks 28
Homemade lemonade 37
Homemade linen water 59
Homemade tomato sauce 93
How to care for mushrooms 193
How to dry roses 78
How to make a dahlia block 126–7
How to press flowers 81
hyacinths 27
hydrangeas 113

I
Infused olive oil 186
irises 27

K
kale 27, 28
   Kale Caesar salad 137
   preparation 28
   Pumpkin table 133

L
labelling 152–3
lamb chops with herbs and spices,
   Grilled 106
laundry tips 154–5
lemonade, Homemade 37
Lemon and rosemary olive oil cake
   184
Lemon butter 34
lemons 31
   cleaning with lemons 38, 50
   food preparation 38
   Homemade lemonade 37
   Infused olive oil 186
   Lemon and rosemary olive oil cake
      184
   Lemon butter 34
   Lemon table 32–3
   Preserved lemons 37
   The perfect roast chicken 44–5
Lemon table 32–3
lilacs 27
Lime dressing 137
lupins 28

M
Make your own flower preserve 29
marigolds 28
Meringue mushrooms 202

mint 27
   Passionfruit Mojito 25
   Pisco Sour 99
mojito, Passionfruit 25
moss 42, 55, 172
Mushroom and pancetta spaghetti
   201
Mushroom feta tart 201
mushrooms 189
   A whimsical mushroom table set-
      ting 190-1
   common mushroom types 192
   How to care for mushrooms 193
   Mushroom and pancetta spaghetti
      201
   Mushroom feta tart 201
   Mushroom pizza 196–7
   Pickled mushrooms 194

O
olive oil
   Garlic confit 198
   Infused olive oil 186
   Lemon and rosemary olive oil cake
      184
olives 179
   A picnic in the olive grove 180
   Olive tapenade 183
   olive types 187
   Yummy olive bread 183
Orchids on the table 170–1
orchids 169
   Orchids on the table 170–1
   potted orchid tips 173
   repotting 172–3
   Whiskey bar 175
organisation 57, 147
   dressing room 158–9
   kitchen 148–9
   laundry 154–5
   office 208–9
   pantry 152–3

P
painting cutlery 24
pancetta spaghetti, Mushroom and
   201
pansies 42
   How to press flowers 81
pantry tips 153
Passionfruit Mojito 25
pattern 20, 54, 96
Peruvian barbecue 95
Peruvian green sauce 107
Pickled mushrooms 194
Pisco Sour 99
Pizza dough 196
pizza, Mushroom 196–7
place cards 24, 33
plates 32, 68, 85, 133

Pollo a la brasa (Grilled chicken)
   104
poppies 28
posies 24, 26–7
   arranging 27
   bulking out 27
potatoes, Thyme and crispy shallot
   104
potting mix 19, 173
potpourri 78
preserve, flower 29
Preserved lemons 37
projects
   Build a nest egg 46–7
   Create a masculine office space
      208–9
   Display your collections in clusters
      150
   Freshen up your bedroom 54–5
   Get creative with autumn leaves
      145
   How to dry roses 78
   How to make a dahlia block 126–7
   How to press flowers 81
   The guest room 56–7
   Washing your woolies 156
   Whiskey bar 175
Pumpkin table 133

Q
Quinoa, avocado and sweet corn
   salad 103

R
ricotta tarts, Tomato and 93
Roasted root vegetable salad 135
roasting times for vegetables 134
rosemary 27
   Infused olive oil 186
   Lemon and rosemary olive oil cake
      184
   fragrant fires 213
   The perfect roast chicken 44–5
roses 67
   A summer romance 68–9
   Extend the life of roses 79
   How to dry roses 78
   Rose cocktail 77
   Rose tea 77
   The semi-naked cake 72–5
rum
   Passionfruit Mojito 25

S
salads
   Avocado, tomato and cheese salad
      102
   Kale Caesar salad 137
   Quinoa, avocado and sweet corn
      salad 103
   Roasted root vegetable salad 135

sauces
  Homemade tomato sauce 93
  Peruvian green sauce 107
settings
  A green thumb's birthday 84–5
  A picnic in the olive grove 180
  A summer romance 68–9
  A whimsical mushroom table setting
    190–1
  Autumnal crunch 140–1
  Feather your nest 42–3
  Lemon table 32–3
  Orchids on the table 170–1
  outdoor 42, 68, 84, 96, 110, 124,
    139, 140, 180
  Pumpkin table 133
  Spring blossom table 20–4
  styling tip 192
  Summer sunshine 110–11
  Tea among the dahlias 124–5
  Welcome to Peru 96–7
Simple sugar syrup 75, **99**, 176
snowballs 28
spaghetti, Mushroom and pancetta
  201
Spring blossom table 20–4
stain removers 53
  blood 53
  coffee 53
  deodorant 53
  grass 53
  grease 53
  ink 53
  lipstick 53
  makeup 53
  oil 53
  red wine 53
  sweat 53
stems 28
  cutting 79
  hearty 28
  hollow 28
  milky 28
  searing 28
  soft 28
  splitting 28
  woody 28
storage 148–9, 150, 152–3, 154–5,
  160–1
Summer sunshine 110–1

T
tapenade, Olive 183
tarts
  Mushroom feta tart 201
  Tomato and ricotta tarts 93
Tea among the dahlias 124–5
tea, Rose 77
The perfect roast chicken 42, 44–5

The perfect roast vegetables 134
The perfect spring posy 26–7
The semi-naked cake 72–5
  tips 75
Thyme and crispy shallot potatoes
  104
thyme 27
  The perfect roast chicken 44–5
  Thyme and crispy shallot potatoes
    104
Tomato and ricotta tarts 93
tomatoes 83
  A green thumb's birthday 84–5
  Avocado, tomato and cheese salad
    102
  Bloody Mary 90
  Homemade tomato sauce 93
  tips for ripening tomatoes 89
  Tomato and ricotta tarts 93
  varieties 88
tulips 28
  preparation 28

V
vases 68, 145, 150, 171
vegetable salad, Roasted root 135
vegetables, The perfect roast 134
vinegar 50
  Pickled mushrooms 194
violets 81
  How to press flowers 81
vodka
  Bloody Mary 90

W
Washing your woolies 156
watering 19, 89, 173
Welcome to Peru 96–7
whiskey
  Espresso Old Fashioned 176
  Whiskey bar 175
Whiskey bar 175
wrapping paper 144

Y
Yummy olive bread 183